He Was
CRUCIFIED

Reflections on the
Passion of Christ

He Was CRUCIFIED

*Reflections on the
Passion of Christ*

Written by

Gerard Joseph Stanley Sr., MD

Edited with annotation by

Kent Jorgen Burreson, PhD

Published by Concordia Publishing House
3558 S. Jefferson Ave., St. Louis, MO 63118-3968
1-800-325-3040 · www.cph.org

Manufactured in China

Library of Congress Cataloging-in-Publication Data
Stanley, Gerard Joseph.
  He was crucified : reflections on the Passion of Christ / written by Gerard Joseph Stanley ; edited with annotation by Kent Burreson.
    p. cm.
  ISBN-13: 978-0-7586-1315-8
  ISBN-10: 0-7586-1315-6
  1. Jesus Christ—Passion. 2. Jesus Christ—Crucifixion. I. Burreson, Kent. II. Title.
  BT431.3.S73 2008
  232.96—dc22   2008028894

1 2 3 4 5 6 7 8 9 10   18 17 16 15 14 13 12 11 10 09

"The exegete cannot afford to neglect any means that may give him a better understanding of the nature and background of the gospel testimony." (*A New Catholic Commentary on Holy Scripture*, 638-a)

I have lectured for more than twenty years on the events of the Passion of Jesus Christ. I would like to thank my wife, Midge; my children: Gerard Stanley Jr., MD, and his lovely wife, Melissa, my daughter, Katy, and her wonderful husband, Matthew Pierson, and my sons Michael and Chuck Stanley; and all my precious grandchildren for their unending support and encouragement throughout the years. They have witnessed firsthand my passion for spreading the word about what Jesus Christ underwent for our sins. I must also thank Father Harry McAlpine for his encouragement to follow my dreams. It is for my family and friends that this book has been written.

—Gerard Joseph Stanley Sr., MD

In thanks for the faith and life of Allen L. Burreson, my sainted father, who lived in Christ Crucified, the Wisdom of God.

—Kent J. Burreson, PhD

Contents

Ways to Use

He Was Crucified

This devotional book can be used anytime during the Church Year to reflect on the Passion of the Lord Jesus Christ. It would be particularly appropriate to read this book during the seasons of Lent and Holy Week. If the book is read during Lent, the Passion accounts from the Gospels can be read in association with each chapter: Matthew with chapter 1, Mark with chapter 2, Luke with chapter 3, and John with chapter 4. In addition, readings, prayers, and hymns for the seasons of Lent and Holy Week appear in each chapter and associate each chapter with a day of Holy Week: chapter 1 with Holy Monday, chapter 2 with Holy Tuesday, chapter 3 with Holy Wednesday, the first two sections of chapter 4 with Holy (Maundy) Thursday, the last two sections of chapter 4 with Good Friday, and chapter 5 with Holy Saturday. Thus the book, along with reading the appropriate Gospels, can enliven the faith of Christians as they journey through Holy Week to the cross and resurrection.

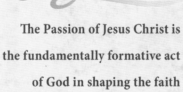

The Passion of Jesus Christ is the fundamentally formative act of God in shaping the faith and life of Christians.

Lord Jesus, in agony
in the garden of Olives,
troubled by sadness and fear,
comforted by an angel:
Have mercy, O Lord, have mercy on us!

Lord Jesus, betrayed by Judas' kiss,
abandoned by your apostles,
delivered into the hands of sinners:
Have mercy, O Lord, have mercy on us!

Lord Jesus, accused by false witnesses,
condemned to die on the cross,
struck by servants, covered with spittle:
Have mercy, O Lord, have mercy on us!

Lord Jesus, disowned by Peter, your apostle,
delivered to Pilate and Herod,
counted among the likes of Barabbas:
Have mercy, O Lord, have mercy on us!

Lord Jesus, carrying your cross to Calvary,
consoled by the daughters of Jerusalem,
helped by Simon of Cyrene:
Have mercy, O Lord, have mercy on us!

Lord Jesus, stripped of your clothes,
given vinegar to drink,
crucified with thieves:
Have mercy, O Lord, have mercy on us!

Lord Jesus, insulted on the cross,
praying for your executioners,
pardoning the good thief:
Have mercy, O Lord, have mercy on us!

Lord Jesus, entrusting your mother
to your beloved disciple,
giving up your spirit into the hands
of your Father, dying for all of us sinners:
Have mercy, O Lord, have mercy on us!

By your sufferings, Lord,
heal the wounds in our hearts.
Let your tears be the source of joy for us,
and let your death give us life.

—Lucien Deiss

9

10 From Jesus' triumphal entry (upper left corner), throughout the various trials, to Golgotha, and to the empty tomb (upper right corner), Hans Memling paints the city of Jerusalem as the backdrop for the Passion story. With the residents of Jerusalem, relive the events of the world's salvation.

Preface

Upon the cross extended
See, world, your Lord suspended.
Your Savior yields His breath.
The Prince of Life from heaven
Himself has freely given
To shame and blows and bitter death.

In his article "On the Physical Death of Jesus Christ," Dr. William Edwards of the Mayo Clinic and two collaborators discuss the medical aspects of crucifixion in an attempt to prove that Jesus Christ died on the cross as His followers and historians claim. Dr. Edwards's article inspired me to educate others on the realities and significance of Jesus' crucifixion. Along my journey, I have come to realize how little I appreciated what Jesus experienced for me as He suffered and died. I have pondered the extreme anguish Jesus experienced in the Garden of Gethsemane. And I have considered the possibility that Jesus may have already experienced in the garden what would happen to Him in His Passion. I comprehend more fully why Jesus asked His Father to take the cup of suffering and death from Him. Through my training and practice as a medical doctor, I can grasp how terribly He suffered at the hands of the Roman guards as they whipped and scourged Him in the Fortress of Antonia.

May this Saxon prayer prepare you for the journey.

Lord Jesus Christ, for the sake of thy holy cross, be with me to shield me. Lord Jesus Christ, by the memory of thy blessed cross, be within me to strengthen me. Lord Jesus Christ, for thy holy cross, be ever round about me to protect me. Lord Jesus Christ, for thy glorious cross, go before me to direct my steps. Lord Jesus Christ, for thy adorable cross, come thou after me to guard me. Lord Jesus Christ, for thy cross, worthy of all praise, overshadow me to bless me. Lord Jesus Christ, for thy noble cross, be thou in me to lead me to thy kingdom. Amen.

I believe that Christians are not fully aware of the agony and anguish that Jesus experienced in the hours following the Last Supper. What happened immediately prior to His crucifixion gives insight into the physical and emotional intensity of Jesus' suffering. Christian faith can be strengthened by reflection upon Christ's suffering both before and during the crucifixion. That is the purpose of this book!

Within these pages, I reflect on the Passion of Jesus Christ in light of the "medical aspects of crucifixion." I invite you to reflect with me on what Jesus endured during the final days of His life. Consider the intensity of His anguish after the Last Supper and ask: What intense emotions would cause Jesus to sweat blood and to ask His Father for help? Reflect with me on the cruelty and severity of Jesus' scourging and beatings, which destroyed the otherwise healthy body of a thirty-three-year-old man, leading to death in a short time on the cross. Finally, reflect on the excruciating nature of the Passion itself. What does it *really* mean to be crucified? Jesus' robes were stripped from His bloodied and torn body. He was thrown to the ground, His hands and feet were nailed to the cross, and He was hung upon it to die. Each word Jesus spoke to His followers while suspended from the cross brought increased pain. Reflect with me on the agony of death by crucifixion.

> And being in an agony He prayed more earnestly; and His sweat became like great drops of blood falling down to the ground.
>
> *Luke 22:44*

Clearly Jesus underwent several remarkable events during His last two days on this earth. As a physician, I find the physical and emotional nature of Jesus' agony in the Garden of Gethsemane, the severity of His scourging at the pillar, and the reality of death by crucifixion to be intellectually, emotionally, and spiritually strengthening for a life of faith in the Crucified One. Reflections on these events through the eyes of a family physician give a unique perspective to the physical and emotional trauma Jesus experienced. In this way, I hope to give you a much clearer and deeper understanding and meaning of what Jesus endured in His arrest, trial, beating, and crucifixion.

Every time I reflect on Jesus' Passion, I grow in my appreciation of what my Savior endured for me and my sins. As you reflect on the events of those two days presented in this book, I hope you, too, will meditate a little longer on the words and artistic depictions of the Passion. If you receive insight into Christ's suffering, then this book has accomplished its purpose. Please join me in reflecting upon the significance of Jesus' suffering as we journey through the Passion of our Lord Jesus Christ.

This carving by William C. Severson depicts Saint Luke—described by Paul as the "beloved physician"—as both physician and biblical writer. His authorship of the third Gospel and the Acts of the Apostles is indicated by the traditional pose of the author presenting his writing.

The raven perched on Luke's shoulder is a Greek symbol of the medical profession. In ancient times, the "dumb" creature that speaks became associated with Greek oracle health shrines, where under the guise of miracles a rather scientific approach to medicine was practiced. The circle on the bracelet on Luke's left wrist is a Christian symbol of the perfection of God. It is also a symbol of the Greek god Apollo, to whom the shrines of healing were most often dedicated.

A fish shape outlines the figure of Luke, which suggests the encompassing effect of Christ, the great fish who swallowed up sickness and death, on Luke, the trained Greek physician.

Introduction

Come, see these things and ponder,
Your soul will fill with wonder
As blood streams from each pore.
Through grief beyond all knowing
From His great heart came flowing
Sighs welling from its deepest core.

This book begins with an examination of the historical context for the Passion of Christ. The lens through which we see this context is the four books of the New Testament that detail the Passion: the Gospels of Matthew, Mark, Luke, and John.

The Passion of our Lord Jesus Christ deals with four different, yet related, events that occur on the final days of Christ's life. These four events are the agony in the Garden of Gethsemane, the scourging at the pillar, the bearing of the cross, and the crucifixion. These events take place in three distinct time periods during the last days of Jesus' earthly life: from the Last Supper to the arrest; from the arrest to the crucifixion at Golgotha; and from the crucifixion at Golgotha to the burial. As we follow these events through the stages of Christ's Passion, we see what Jesus endured to redeem our lives from sin and deliver us into new life through His resurrection.

Jesus' agony and the serious intent of our Savior's prayer to the Father are the focus of this woodcut by Albrecht Dürer. Even as Jesus prays for the Father's will to be done, an angel holds the cross before His face.

The first stage of His Passion, the agony in the Garden of Gethsemane, gives Jesus the initial experience of the suffering He will endure. To appreciate the intensity of His agony, we re-create the timeline for that night, then examine the suffering and grief Jesus experienced on the night before His death. In the garden, Jesus foresees the cruel torture He will endure. Already, this first taste of suffering necessitates that Jesus receive strength and support from an angel of God. To grasp the nature of His agony in the garden, we must ask, *What did Jesus experience that was so emotionally intense that it caused His sweat to be like blood?*

During the second stage of His Passion (from His arrest until His crucifixion), Jesus endured two events of severe torture and pain: the scourging at the pillar and the bearing of the cross. An inhumane practice, scourging was the beating of a condemned victim in preparation for death. This practice was so hostile that a soldier was charged with ensuring that the victim did not die as a result of the beating. To comprehend the pain experienced by the condemned victim, we must ask, *How extreme would the beating be to destroy a thirty-three-year-old man's body, subsequently leading to death in a very short time on the cross?* The Shroud of Turin, discussed in the appendix, points to potential answers. It shows a victim that had been severely scourged over most of his body. Large bruises also show that the victim carried a heavy crossbeam across his shoulders. Our review of scourging will demonstrate the cruelty unleashed on Jesus and help us realize why He died so quickly on the cross.

In Albrecht Dürer's depiction of the scourging at the pillar, Jesus appears strong and healthy, though the vicious punishment to come will erode His vitality. The faces of the soldiers reveal the malicious nature of this torture.

Following the scourging is the third event of the Passion of our Lord: the bearing of the cross ("the way of the cross") as Jesus is led from His condemnation before Pilate to His place of execution. The public humiliation associated with Jesus' bearing His own cross inflicted further emotional and physical torture on Him and on those who loved Him, including His mother and His followers.

These first three events of Christ's Passion prepare for the fourth event, which completes the final stage of His Passion: the crucifixion. In this ultimate humiliation and torture, Christ accepts the most degrading insults to His human body and so, along with His resurrection, frees us from our sins. So that our faith in His atoning Passion might be strengthened, we must ask, *What does it really mean to be crucified?* The crucifixion of Jesus must be placed into its historical context as a form of capital punishment. The physiological effects of crucifixion caused the victim extreme pain, even as this torture brought about a slow and painful death. Breathing and talking were excruciating, thus we should treasure the words Jesus spoke as He was dying. The final humiliation for the Son of God was the act that certified His death—the spear plunged into His side. By contemplating the final act of His Passion, we will know more intimately the depth of Jesus' love for us, in whose place He suffered and died.

The emotional and physical impact of Jesus' Passion is apparent in Albrecht Dürer's image of Christ bearing the cross. Having fallen in weakness, His face creased with anguish and pain, Jesus looks back with longing love toward His mother and the beloved disciple, John. At the same time, the soldier mercilessly prods Jesus to continue on to Golgotha.

Albrecht Dürer's woodcut of the crucifixion depicts a Jesus who has already succumbed to death. While the soldiers are disinterested and the women weep at the cross, one man—the Roman centurion—raises his hands toward heaven and confesses, "Truly this was the Son of God."

One contemplates the Passion in order to find strength and joy, or as Martin Luther states:

We need to study the passion of Christ, in order that we might remember that it happened for our good and for our eternal benefit. I must have regard for his bloody sweat, his agony, and his crucifixion, and say, That is my help, my strength, my life, my joy. All this happened for our sakes and for our benefit. We must believe this and thank him from the bottom of our hearts. Whoever does that and views the suffering of Christ in this way is a Christian.

Through these pages, you will reflect on the suffering of Jesus from His Last Supper with His disciples to His last breath on the cross. You will reflect on what Jesus experienced during these events. You will reflect on what Jesus experienced while praying in the Garden of Gethsemane. You will reflect on what really happened to Jesus' body as He was scourged in preparation for death. You will reflect on Jesus' experience while bearing His cross to Calvary. You will reflect on the process of being crucified and the torture and pain Jesus suffered while dying on the cross. Finally, you will reflect on the words by which Jesus' cross becomes your life and salvation by faith: "out of the cross" (*excruciatus*) has come the salvation of the world.

The many facets of salvation associated with the cross are summarized in this hymn to the cross by Paulinus, a bishop of Nola in the fourth century.

O Cross, ineffable love of
God and glory of heaven!
O Cross, eternal salvation;
Cross, terror of the reprobate.
O Cross, support of the just,
light of Christians, for you,
God became a slave in the
flesh, here on earth;

by your means, man in God
is crowned king in heaven;

from you streams the
true light, victorious
over accursed night.

You gave believers power
to make the pantheon
of the nations quake;

you are the soul of peace
that unites men in Christ
the mediator;

you are the ladder for man
to climb to heaven.

Be always for us,
your faithful, both pillar
and anchor;

watch over our homes,
set the course of our ship.

In the Cross may our faith
remain strong, and there be
our crown prepared.

As Jesus is presented to the crowds who are seeking to crucify Him, Pilate says, *Ecce, homo*, that is, "Behold, the man." Through your reflection, you are responding to Pilate's call, though not as the Roman governor intended. Rather, you behold Jesus through faith, as this painting by Antonio Ciseri invites you to do.

Chapter One

THrough the Evangelists' Eyes

The Passion of Christ in Historical Context

Allow this prayer to shape your reflection on the meaning of Christ's suffering because of you, in your place, on your behalf. Almighty God, grant that in the midst of our failures and weaknesses we may be restored through the passion and intercession of Your only-begotten Son, who lives and reigns with You and the Holy Spirit, one God, now and forever. Amen.

Who is it, Lord, that bruised You?
Who has so sore abused You
And caused You all Your woe?
We all must make confession
Of sin and dire transgression
While You no ways of evil know.

Faith and trust in the God who reveals Himself in the person and work of Jesus Christ, especially in His Passion and death on the cross, calls for hearing and knowing the Word that bears witness to Him. The apostles of Jesus Christ and their followers preached that Word as the Gospel (*evangelion*), or Good News, that Jesus Christ had risen from the dead. They proclaimed His Passion, death, and resurrection as the way to eternal life and salvation.

The apostles, as those chosen and sent by Jesus, announced the events of His ministry, persecution, death, resurrection, and ascension as the saving work of God. As the numbers of new Christians grew and the apostles aged, were martyred, or died, the need to write down the story and proclamation of Christ Jesus became imperative. The evangelists completed their record of Jesus' life, death, and resurrection by the end of the first century AD, a record that comes to us in the New Testament Gospels.

In *Jesus Christ Blessing*, Spanish painter Ferdinando Gallego surrounds the Savior with four symbols from the first chapter of Revelation, symbols that are traditionally associated with the four evangelists. Beginning in the upper right and moving clockwise, Gallego includes the angel in human form, which symbolizes Matthew, whose Gospel opens with the incarnation and emphasizes Jesus' humanity. The ox symbolizes Luke, who stresses Jesus' sacrifice in his Gospel. Mark's symbol, the winged lion, recalls an ancient legend that lion cubs lie for three days as dead until "resurrected" by their father's breath. His Gospel account emphasizes Jesus' death and resurrection. John is depicted by the eagle because his Gospel soars to the most sublime, spiritual heights.

Jacob Jordaens depicts the unanimity of the four evangelists as they gather around the writing of the Gospel of Jesus Christ. While the historicity of the depiction is hypothetical, the continuity of the Gospel accounts is readily apparent. It is a continuity seen in the Passion of Jesus: the central story of the Messiah told fundamentally with the same stroke of the pen by all four evangelists. One imagines them pondering the pages, recounting the finished work of the cross.

"Drawing on this rich treasure of oral tradition and written narrative, the evangelists, each in his own way . . . set before us the story of Jesus." For approximately three decades after the ascension, the "Good News" was preached and taught by the Church before being written in the form of the Gospels. Although exact timelines and details were not the primary emphasis of the evangelists, the fundamental chronology and details remain constant throughout the four Gospels. Each evangelist presents the events as he or his teachers saw them. Nevertheless, "the theology of the evangelists is no private interpretation but the interpretation presented to us by the first generation of Christians under the inspiration of the Holy Spirit."

The evangelists give us a wondrous account of the events of Jesus' life, suffering, death, and resurrection, but that story had existed before the Gospels were penned. The apostles were the first preachers of the Good News. As we can see, there exist three stages of Gospel proclamation: Jesus Christ Himself, the witness of the apostles to Him, and the written word of the evangelists. It was the apostolic Church that treasured the Gospel that has been handed down to us today according to the viewpoint of each of the Gospel writers. When we consider all three stages of the Gospel's proclamation, we appreciate how the Gospels complement one another in telling the story of the Word made flesh.

Today, we learn of world events from on-the-spot reporting and sound-bite-heavy, scripted interviews, so it is difficult to imagine older ways of obtaining knowledge. To think of learning by word of mouth of events that occurred weeks or years before sounds slow, ineffective, and prone to gaps, errors, and misinterpretations. The development of the written record of the events of Jesus' life and His teaching took place as the eyewitness testimony, the word-of-mouth accounts, and the memories of those who had heard the events were brought together by the inspired evangelists.

Because communication took place by word of mouth and from memory, the similarity of the accounts of Jesus' life, ministry, teaching, and Passion as written by the evangelists is amazing. Different individuals from different perspectives identically record many of the events in Jesus' life and ministry. To put this into perspective, imagine recalling events from five or ten years ago, then telling others about those events, and then later putting on paper these same thoughts. The accomplishments of the apostles and evangelists in accurately recording the teaching and events of Jesus' ministry, Passion, death, and resurrection are amazing evidence of the guidance of the Holy Spirit that was instrumental in the writing of the Gospels.

The first four books of the New Testament—the Gospels according to Matthew, Mark, Luke, and John—contain the story of Jesus Christ and His teaching. The first three Gospels—Matthew, Mark, and Luke—resemble one another in many respects. They are called the Synoptic Gospels because it is often possible to arrange their texts in parallel columns, so as to view them in a single glance (synopsis). John's Gospel differs dramatically in character but shows many similarities to Luke's Gospel in its story line. Despite the differences throughout each of the Gospels, the sections of those books that deal with the Passion of our Lord are remarkably similar (Matthew 26–27; Mark 14:32–15:47; Luke 22–23; John 18–19).

Six days before the Passover, Jesus therefore came to Bethany, where Lazarus was, whom Jesus had raised from the dead. So they gave a dinner for Him there. Martha served, and Lazarus was one of those reclining with Him at the table. Mary therefore took a pound of expensive ointment made from pure nard, and anointed the feet of Jesus and wiped His feet with her hair. The house was filled with the fragrance of the perfume. But Judas Iscariot, one of His disciples (he who was about to betray Him), said, "Why was this ointment not sold for three hundred denarii and given to the poor?" He said this, not because he cared about the poor, but because he was a thief, and having charge of the moneybag he used to help himself to what was put into it. Jesus said, "Leave her alone, so that she may keep it for the day of My burial. The poor you always have with you, but you do not always have Me."

When the large crowd of the Jews learned that Jesus was there, they came, not only on account of Him but also to see Lazarus, whom He had raised from the dead. So the chief priests made plans to put Lazarus to death as well, because on account of him many of the Jews were going away and believing in Jesus.

The next day the large crowd that had come to the feast heard that Jesus was coming to Jerusalem. So they took branches of palm trees and went out to meet Him, crying out, "Hosanna! Blessed is He who comes in the name of the Lord, even the King of Israel!" And Jesus found a young donkey and sat on it, just as it is written,

"Fear not, daughter of Zion; behold, your king is coming, sitting on a donkey's colt!"

His disciples did not understand these things at first, but when Jesus was glorified, then they remembered that these things

had been written about Him and had been done to Him. The crowd that had been with Him when He called Lazarus out of the tomb and raised him from the dead continued to bear witness. The reason why the crowd went to meet Him was that they heard He had done this sign. So the Pharisees said to one another, "You see that you are gaining nothing. Look, the world has gone after Him."

Now among those who went up to worship at the feast were some Greeks. So these came to Philip, who was from Bethsaida in Galilee, and asked him, "Sir, we wish to see Jesus." Philip went and told Andrew; Andrew and Philip went and told Jesus. And Jesus answered them, "The hour has come for the Son of Man to be glorified."

John 12:1–23

Reading the evangelists' accounts of Jesus' Passion lets us enter the final days of His remarkable life. Following Christ's Last Supper, we are taken to the Garden of Gethsemane, where the evangelists portray the anguish Jesus suffered as He accepted what He would soon endure. We hear of the trials and physical abuse that Jesus underwent at the hands of the Jews and then the Romans. The horror and cruelty of the moment are revealed in the account of Jesus' bearing the cross and in His subsequent crucifixion. The written accounts of the last three days of Jesus' life provide only a glimpse into the horror and fear that the apostles experienced while witnessing Jesus' arrest, trials, beatings, and death. "The apostles, companions of Jesus during His public ministry [and] witnesses of His death and of His glorification . . . after those events understood more clearly—had seen in a new light—what their Master had said and done. Now that He had entered into His glory and that they had been enlightened by the Spirit of God, they at last grasped who and what He was: it is their witness and their preaching which come to us through the written Gospels."

Through the Gospel accounts, we enter into the final days of Christ's life. Like the pilgrims in Jerusalem for the Passover, we join the throng entering Jerusalem with Jesus, who was humbly riding a donkey to His enthronement on the wood of the cross. Here Benjamin Robert Haydon captures the adoration of the crowds who cried, "Hosanna to the Son of David!"

By following the order that the Gospels appear in the Bible, we can examine the unique perspective of each evangelist, especially as that perspective shapes the Passion story. Matthew's Gospel has a profoundly Jewish character, reflecting its first-century Jewish author. In his writing, Matthew reflects the influence of rabbinical forms of dialogue, as well as the basic premise that Christ's mission was to the Jews. The Christ, or Messiah, was to be the son of David, heir to the Davidic throne, promised to Israel as its Savior. As a result, Matthew's narrative of the Passion is shaped significantly by the fulfillment in Jesus of the Old Testament prophecies of the Messiah who would redeem Israel. The central theme of the Passion in Matthew's Gospel is the ultimate exultation of God's servant Messiah through His suffering. As the servant Messiah, Jesus' calm foreknowledge and complete acceptance and resignation to His Passion is emphasized repeatedly by Matthew.

In Rembrandt's etching, the heavenly light shining on the crucified Messiah depicts God's acceptance of His suffering. This light also encompasses the repentant thief and the centurion, who is kneeling as he acknowledges Jesus as the Son of God. Recall the words of the prophet Micah: "Rejoice not over me, O my enemy; when I fall, I shall rise; when I sit in darkness, the LORD will be a light to me" (Micah 7:8).

The Lord GOD has opened
my ear,
    and I was not rebellious;
    I turned not backward.
I gave my back to those
who strike,
    and my cheeks to those who
    pull out the beard;
I hid not my face
    from disgrace and spitting.

But the Lord GOD helps me;
    therefore I have not
    been disgraced;
therefore I have set my face
like a flint,
    and I know that I shall not
    be put to shame.
He who vindicates me
is near.

Who will contend with me?
    Let us stand up together.
Who is my adversary?
    Let him come near to me.
Behold, the Lord GOD helps me;
    who will declare me guilty?
Behold, all of them will wear out
like a garment;
    the moth will eat them up.

Who among you fears the LORD
    and obeys the voice of
    His servant?
Let him who walks in darkness
    and has no light
trust in the name of the LORD
    and rely on his God.

Isaiah 50:5–10

Now the chief priests and the whole Council were seeking testimony against Jesus to put Him to death, but they found none. For many bore false witness against Him, but their testimony did not agree. And some stood up and bore false witness against Him, saying, "We heard Him say, 'I will destroy this temple that is made with hands, and in three days I will build another, not made with hands.'" Yet even about this their testimony did not agree. And the high priest stood up in the midst and asked Jesus, "Have You no answer to make? What is it that these men testify against You?" But He remained silent and made no answer.

Again the high priest asked Him, "Are You the Christ, the Son of the Blessed?" And Jesus said, "I am, and you will see the Son of Man seated at the right hand of Power, and coming with the clouds of heaven." And the high priest tore his garments and said, "What further witnesses do we need? You have heard His blasphemy. What is your decision?" And they all condemned Him as deserving death. And some began to spit on Him and to cover His face and to strike Him, saying to Him, "Prophesy!" And the guards received Him with blows.

Mark 14:55–65

Mark's Gospel has always been viewed as conveying the voice of the apostle Peter as it relates the story of Jesus. While Mark's Gospel does have a Jewish character, it is written also for the benefit of Gentiles. It seeks to demonstrate that Christ was indeed the Son of God.

Yet Mark's narrative emphasizes not only that Jesus is the Son of God but also that He is the Son of Man. The Son of Man, a figure through whom God judges and rules in the Old Testament, is portrayed by Mark as demonstrating His authority through His death and resurrection. The Son of Man is the Messiah who by suffering and dying judges and saves the world and brings it under His final reign.

The Passion narrative is so important to Mark's portrayal of Jesus, the Son of God and Messiah, the suffering Son of Man, that his Gospel is often referred to as a Passion narrative with an extended introduction. This emphasis can be seen in many ways throughout the Gospel. Most obvious is Mark's inclusion of three predictions made by Jesus concerning His coming Passion. Mark also emphasizes the stubbornness of the Jewish leaders who were unwilling to accept Jesus for what He is, thus leading to their decision to have Him killed. In contrast to the leaders, Mark poignantly emphasizes Christ's foreknowledge of and willingness to accept His cruel death. In the process Mark shows the followers of Jesus that they, too, will be called on to suffer as Jesus did.

IHS OVS NAZ ΩΡΑΙΟS ΟΒΑΖ
ΙΕΥΣ ΤΟΝ ΙΟΥΔΑΙΟΝ
IE SVS NAZARAENVS REX IVΕ
ΟRVΜ ✠

Francisco de Zurbaran painted Christ with His head tilted upward toward His heavenly Father. In this subtle cue, believers glimpse Christ's willingness to accept His suffering at the hands of humanity in order to fulfill the will of His Father. God's will is to have mercy on sinners. In turning the other cheek on the cross, Jesus is God's mercy to humanity.

29

Luke wrote his Gospel, the Gospel most reflective of a Gentile audience, in the region of Achaia while a disciple of the apostles. A Syrian of Antioch, Luke traveled extensively with Paul. A physician, Luke's use of the Greek language is considered the best among the evangelists and probably was his native tongue. Not only was Luke a gifted writer, but he was also, according to tradition, a poet and artist. Having proven himself an artist with words, Luke traditionally receives credit for painting the first icon of the Virgin Mary. Regardless of the veracity of this claim, Luke's poetic and artistic description of the story of Christ has inspired Christian artists throughout the ages.

The gentle heart apparent in Luke's Gospel enabled him to pay careful attention to the women who were such an integral part of Jesus' life. For example, as he describes Jesus bearing the cross, Luke mentions the women of Jerusalem, on whom Jesus, even in His final torturous hours, takes pity because He knows the suffering they will face. Luke portrays Jesus as the Savior who has complete compassion, tenderness, and unrestricted forgiveness.

In Jacopo Tintoretto's painting, it appears as if all of humanity has gathered around the cross, bent on destroying the Son of God. Yet the outstretched arms of Jesus and the light emanating from Him reveal He is in control and intent on gathering all people to Himself.

Luke's Gospel of mercy and pardon is the Gospel of the Supreme Physician of souls who has told us "the son of man came to seek and to save the lost" (Luke 19:10). The Lord, who is hailed as "Savior" at His birth, saves the lost through the salvation accomplished in His death and resurrection. Yet Christ's Passion for sinners was not without cost. He suffered greatly, as Luke shows us, especially in the anguish of His soul. In the Garden of Gethsemane, Jesus is troubled because having mercy on humanity will lead Him into the jaws of suffering and death. This spiritual anguish affects Jesus physically, causing His sweat to become like "great drops of blood" (Luke 22:44).

An angel of heaven provided the spiritual support and strength Jesus needed to endure this struggle to be the righteous Son of God. Yet as Luke makes clear, during His arrest, trials, scourging, and crucifixion, Jesus at all times remained in perfect command of Himself and of what was happening to Him.

And when they came to the place that is called The Skull, there they crucified Him, and the criminals, one on His right and one on His left. And Jesus said, "Father, forgive them, for they know not what they do." And they cast lots to divide His garments. And the people stood by, watching, but the rulers scoffed at Him, saying, "He saved others; let Him save Himself, if He is the Christ of God, His Chosen One!"

Luke 23:33–35

And when He came to the place, He said to them, "Pray that you may not enter into temptation." And He withdrew from them about a stone's throw, and knelt down and prayed, saying, "Father, if You are willing, remove this cup from Me. Nevertheless, not My will, but Yours, be done." And there appeared to Him an angel from heaven, strengthening Him. And being in an agony He prayed more earnestly; and His sweat became like great drops of blood falling down to the ground. And when He rose from prayer, He came to the disciples and found them sleeping for sorrow, and He said to them, "Why are you sleeping? Rise and pray that you may not enter into temptation."

Luke 22:40–46

Lucas Cranach the Elder draws us into the drama of the crucifixion, placing us on the same level as Mary and John, the beloved disciple. Along with these closest witnesses of Jesus' Passion, we see the mystery of Christ's cross as the mystery of His glory, the darkness of the sky giving way to the brightness of salvation and eternal life within the family of God. In His beloved, crucified Son the Father is well pleased.

33

For Saint John, then, Christ's cross and death are unintelligible unless they are seen as a sign of his glorification and exaltation. . . . In St. John's gospel, the cross itself is presented as resurrection and glory no less than as death. John certainly depicts the crucifixion as a visible, sensibly real event, but he also insists that it be seen as a sign that contains what it signifies, namely, Christ's glorification. When Christ is dying, he is already going back to the Father.

—Adrian Nocent

The key to Byzantine icons is the cross. Even if not explicitly depicted, the icon's focal point is cruciform or cross-shaped because the cross is at the center of the relationship between God and the believer. In this icon, the merciful compassion of Jesus in giving His disciple John and His mother, Mary, into each other's care calls us to show one another this same compassion that flows from the One who is crucified but abounding in mercy.

John's Gospel provides an intimate portrait of the life and ministry of Jesus of Nazareth. The apostle John, along with his brother, James, was one of the two sons of Zebedee and was raised to be a fisherman. Most likely John is the "beloved disciple" of Jesus mentioned often in this Gospel. Certainly John was part of the inner circle of apostles and an eyewitness to Christ's life, ministry, Passion, and resurrection. As the beloved disciple, John probably was seated closest to Jesus during the Last Supper, and he was present at Gethsemane and at the Jewish trial of Jesus. We know from the Gospel's account that Jesus entrusted His mother to John, which means John witnessed the crucifixion.

In both style and message, John's Gospel contrasts with the Synoptic Gospels as it reveals the glory of Jesus as the Son of God who makes known the Father and His salvation. Belief in Jesus as the one sent by the Father to save the world provides those who trust in Him with eternal life and salvation. Yet with regard to the Passion, John's account is almost identical to the accounts found in the Synoptic Gospels. Throughout the Passion, John depicts Jesus as the Son of God, sent from the Father, who fulfills the Father's will.

Now among those who went up to worship at the feast were some Greeks. So these came to Philip, who was from Bethsaida in Galilee, and asked him, "Sir, we wish to see Jesus." Philip went and told Andrew; Andrew and Philip went and told Jesus. And Jesus answered them, "The hour has come for the Son of Man to be glorified. Truly, truly, I say to you, unless a grain of wheat falls into the earth and dies, it remains alone; but if it dies, it bears much fruit. Whoever loves his life loses it, and whoever hates his life in this world will keep it for eternal life. If anyone serves Me, he must follow Me; and where I am, there will My servant be also. If anyone serves Me, the Father will honor him. "Now is My soul troubled. And what shall I say? 'Father, save Me from this hour'? But for this purpose I have come to this hour. Father, glorify Your name." Then a voice came from heaven: "I have glorified it, and I will glorify it again." The crowd that stood there and heard it said that it had thundered. Others said, "An angel has spoken to Him." Jesus answered, "This voice has come for your sake, not Mine. Now is the judgment of this world; now will the ruler of this world be cast out. And I, when I am lifted up from the earth, will draw all people to Myself." He said this to show by what kind of death He was going to die.

John 12:20–33

As you pray this prayer, rejoice that each Gospel account tells this same story: by His cross Jesus overcomes death and the grave and by His resurrection brings life and salvation to light.

It is truly good, right, and salutary that we should at all times and in all places give thanks to You, holy Lord, almighty Father, everlasting God, through Jesus Christ, our Lord, who on this day overcame death and the grave and by His glorious resurrection opened to us the way of everlasting life. Therefore with angels and archangels and with all the company of heaven we laud and magnify Your glorious name, evermore praising You.

Jesus comes with authority and power as witnessed in His cry from the cross, "It is finished," which indicated that He had fulfilled the Father's will to save His human creatures. In His victorious death, we know this Jesus to be the Christ—the promised Messiah—the very Son of God, the one in whom we must believe. The Passion, death, and resurrection of Christ Jesus are at the center of all four Gospels and shape the narrative of each book. While Jesus' Passion is central to the Gospels, the details of the suffering He endured and the specifics of crucifixion are not. The evangelists do not dwell on the frightful tortures of crucifixion. After all, the earliest Christians were all too familiar with the horrific nature of this form of capital punishment and what preceded it. The evangelists' purpose was to show how the events of the Lord's Passion fulfilled the Scriptures and were the proclamation of God's mercy in His Son, the very salvation of the world.

Christ of Saint John of the Cross by Salvador Dalí, one of the most reproduced paintings of the twentieth century, demonstrates that the Gospel writers did not focus on the horrific details of Christ's Passion. Dali depicts Christ as the beautiful Son of God in human flesh that He is, and this beauty reflects the purpose of the Gospels to proclaim the Passion of Christ as the beautiful, saving, and redeeming work of God.

Paschal Lamb,
by God appointed,
All our sins on Thee were laid;
By almighty love anointed,
Thou hast full atonement made.
All Thy people are forgiven
Through the virtue
of Thy blood;
Opened is the gate of heaven,
Reconciled are we with God.

Jesus, hail! Enthroned in glory,
There forever to abide;
All the heav'nly hosts
adore Thee,
Seated at Thy Father's side.
There for sinners
Thou art pleading;

There Thou dost our
place prepare,
Ever for us
interceding
Till in glory we appear.

Worship, honor,
pow'r, and blessing
Thou art worthy to receive;
Highest praises,
without ceasing,
Right it is for us to give.
Help, ye bright angelic spirits,
All your noblest anthems raise;
Help to sing our Savior's merits,
Help to chant
Immanuel's praise!

Chapter Two

THe Suffering of Jesus Christ

From the Last Supper to the Arrest

I caused Your grief and sighing
By evils multiplying
As countless as the sands.
I caused the woes unnumbered
With which Your soul is cumbered,
Your sorrows raised by wicked hands.

The events that took place in the Garden of Gethsemane on the final night of Jesus' life are mentioned in each of the Gospel accounts of the Passion of Christ. All too often these events are reflected upon briefly in an effort to move quickly to the crucifixion and resurrection. Yet understanding what Jesus went through in the Garden of Gethsemane sets the emotional and physical tone for the rest of His life-ending ordeal. I believe it is key for Christians to understand the events of that night and how Jesus felt about and approached His death.

This first stage of the Passion, the agony in the Garden of Gethsemane, begs the question: What did Jesus experience in the garden that caused Him to sweat like blood (a condition called *hemohidrosis*)? Other than prayer, what occurred in those few hours in the middle of the night? How long were Jesus and His disciples in the garden? How long did He suffer from hemohidrosis and experience even then the full depth of the pain to come? Allow these questions to guide your reflection on what Jesus endured in the Garden of Gethsemane that night more than two thousand years ago.

Reflecting on the Passion of Christ is intended not simply to lead to a better understanding of what happened to Christ but to strengthen your faith in the mercy of God made known in Christ's Passion.

Almighty and everlasting God, grant us by Your grace so to pass through this holy time of our Lord's passion that we may obtain the forgiveness of our sins; through Jesus Christ, Your Son, our Lord, who lives and reigns with You and the Holy Spirit, one God, now and forever. Amen.

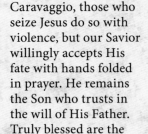

In this painting by Caravaggio, those who seize Jesus do so with violence, but our Savior willingly accepts His fate with hands folded in prayer. He remains the Son who trusts in the will of His Father. Truly blessed are the meek, for they will inherit the earth.

The song of praise sung by the Palm Sunday crowds, commonly referred to as the Sanctus and still sung by many Christians in worship, praises Jesus, the one sent by God to establish His kingdom through suffering, death, and resurrection.

Holy, holy, holy

Lord God of power
and might:

Heaven and earth
are full of Your glory.

Hosanna in the highest.

Blessed is He who comes
in the name of the Lord.

Hosanna in the highest.

The Events in the Garden

In reviewing the events that followed the Last Supper, much effort has been devoted to establishing a timeline for Christ's Passion. Less attention has been paid to the timeline of events that took place in the Garden of Gethsemane. Following the Supper, Jesus and His disciples left the Upper Room in the city of Jerusalem where they had celebrated the Passover. They walked together through the city walls and across the Kidron Valley to the Garden of Gethsemane on the Mount of Olives.

This walk would have led Jesus and the disciples through throngs of people who had come to the Holy City for the high feast of Passover. Jerusalem had swelled from a population of around 25,000 to more than 300,000 people within the city walls and in the surrounding countryside. Most likely Jesus and His disciples would have walked amid thousands of people. The countryside would have been ablaze with countless campfires. Religious excitement would have filled the air. Only a few days earlier, Jesus, along with the disciples, had been paraded into the city accompanied by shouts of praise to the God of Israel, their Savior and King.

At the far right of this painting by Pietro Lorenzetti, a man reaches to break off a palm branch, which he will add to those at the donkeys' feet. An ancient sign of victory and kingship, the palm branches witness the acclamation, "Blessed is the King who comes in the name of the Lord," which accompanied the Messiah's entry into Jerusalem (Luke 19:38). These palm branches would become signs of suffering and martyrdom, signs of Jesus' Passion, His enthronement as the King of Israel.

The sarcophagus (burial chamber) of Junius Bassus (ca. AD 359) includes this image of Christ entering Jerusalem on a donkey. The pilgrims in Jerusalem wave palm branches in acclamation and line His way with their garments. What may seem an inappropriate image for a sarcophagus is actually a fitting choice for the resting chamber of a Christian. Jesus entered Jerusalem to walk the way of the cross, the way of His suffering and death. In so doing, Jesus opened the way to eternal life with His heavenly Father for those who believe on His name.

The apostles would have been filled with pride and excitement as their friend, teacher, and leader assumed what they believed to be His rightful place as the Messiah and longed-for deliverer of Israel. Yet the events of Holy Week—and especially the events and revelations of this particular night—would have left them astounded and perplexed.

After the Supper, more questions would have been raised than answers given. Most likely, the disciples would have thought, if not asked: Why did Jesus turn over the tables of the money changers and run people out of the temple? What did Jesus mean when He talked of betrayal? Why did Jesus tell Peter, of all people, that he would deny knowing Him? What did Jesus mean when He said the bread was His body and the wine His blood? What did Jesus mean when He said we would not see Him, and then in a little while we would see Him? Why was Jesus talking about leaving and sending the Helper when He returns to His heavenly Father? These and other questions would have generated conversation among the eleven men following Jesus to His place of prayer.

For the word of the cross is folly to those who are perishing, but to us who are being saved it is the power of God. For it is written,

> *"I will destroy the wisdom of the wise,*
>
> *and the discernment of the discerning I will thwart."*

Where is the one who is wise? Where is the scribe? Where is the debater of this age? Has not God made foolish the wisdom of the world? For since, in the wisdom of God, the world did not know God through wisdom, it pleased God through the folly of what we preach to save those who believe. For Jews demand signs and Greeks seek wisdom, but we preach Christ crucified, a stumbling block to Jews and folly to Gentiles, but to those who are called, both Jews and Greeks, Christ the power of God and the wisdom of God. For the foolishness of God is wiser than men, and the weakness of God is stronger than men.

For consider your calling, brothers: not many of you were wise according to worldly standards, not many were powerful, not many were of noble birth. But God chose what is foolish in the world to shame the wise; God chose what is weak in the world to shame the strong; God chose what is low and despised in the world, even things that are not, to bring to nothing things that are, so that no human being might boast in the presence of God. He is the source of your life in Christ Jesus, whom God made our wisdom and our righteousness and sanctification and redemption. Therefore, as it is written, "Let the one who boasts, boast in the Lord."

1 Corinthians 1:18–31

According to Jerome, a fourth-century theologian, we find ourselves mirrored in the weakness of the disciples as they wait with Jesus in His agony.

"Watch and pray that you may not enter into temptation." It is impossible for the human soul to avoid temptation. Hence we say in the Lord's Prayer, "Lead us not into temptation," which we are unable to withstand. We do not refuse to face temptation entirely but pray for the strength to bear up under it. Therefore he does not say, "Watch and pray that you may not be tempted" but "that you may not enter into temptation," that is, that temptation may not overwhelm you and hold you in its grip. For example, a martyr who has shed blood by professing faith in the Lord was certainly tempted but was not ensnared in the net of temptation. One who denies the faith, however, has fallen into the snares of temptation.

"The spirit indeed is willing, but the flesh is weak." This is aimed at those rash people who think that whatever they believe, they can obtain. Therefore, as much as we trust in the ardor of our spirit, so too should we fear the weakness of the flesh. And yet, according to the apostle the works of the flesh are mortified by the Spirit.

From Mark's Gospel, it is apparent that Jesus led the eleven to the Mount of Olives and into the Garden of Gethsemane. Once there, He took three of the disciples—Peter and the two sons of Zebedee, James and John—with Him a short distance from the others. Jesus had talked several times to His disciples about the terrible death He would soon experience, and now Mark points out that Jesus became "greatly distressed and troubled" (14:33).

After asking Peter, James, and John to wait and watch with Him, Jesus moved further from these men to be by Himself. In light of what He knew would happen, Jesus fell on the ground and prayed, "Abba, Father, all things are possible for You.

Remove this cup from Me. Yet not what I will, but what You will" (14:36). The word *Abba* is Aramaic for "father."

Luke indicates that an angel from heaven appeared to strengthen Jesus as His extreme agony led Him to pray even more earnestly. Luke describes Jesus' sweat becoming "like great drops of blood falling down to the ground" (22:44).

The accounts of these events in the Garden of Gethsemane are similar in each of the Gospels. Apparently the three disciples who accompanied Jesus away from the others listened long enough to perceive that Jesus was in deep prayer and very anguished. The Gospels include the disciples'

accounts of Jesus' prayer to His Father, as well as descriptions of Jesus' emotional state—and each evangelist speaks of Jesus' prayer and agony in the same way.

After praying for a period of time, Jesus returned to find His followers asleep. How long did Jesus pray and suffer in agony? Personally, after a meal with friends that includes drinks, a walk around the neighborhood, and stimulating conversation, it may take an hour or longer to feel sleepy enough to end the conversation, lay down, and fall asleep. Although it may have been shorter or longer, Jesus probably remained alone a good hour or more the first time as He prayed and agonized with His Father.

Sebastiano Ricci depicts Jesus' soulful plea to His Father for the cup of His suffering to be removed. The angel holds the cup, bringing it to Jesus and pointing toward the Father. Jesus, His face bowed to the ground, accepts His Father's will, His hand open toward His Father in voluntary submission.

Be awake; do not snore; do not be secure as if you no longer needed to be vigilant. Bear in mind: My worst enemy is closest to me, I am carrying him in my breast. Therefore if God does not help me with His Holy Spirit, I am lost. I cannot govern and sustain myself for a solitary hour. Therefore I will pray God for His Holy Spirit that through Him He may govern and guide me aright and either protect me against trials and temptations or graciously assist me and not permit me to fall. . . . But in order to be safe we must also see to it that our hearts are not "overcharged with surfeiting and drunkenness" (Luke 21:34).

For we have the bad habit of becoming wanton when well fed, as do cattle. He who has an abundance and a sufficiency has soon forgotten God and His Word or pays little attention to God. Then it easily happens that a man walks into the snare of the devil before he is aware of it. Therefore these three things should be conjoined: that you fear God, that you watch and are sober, and that you pray without ceasing. Then you will have no trouble. For though we cannot be entirely relieved of temptations and at times fall because of weakness, God will nonetheless lead us out of the depth through His Holy Spirit. Then we do not continue to lie there.

—*Martin Luther*

Upon returning to the group and finding them asleep, Jesus awakened His disciples and chastised them for not being able to stay awake for even one hour. Presumably He talked to them for a short period of time before removing Himself again to continue praying. According to Matthew and Mark, Jesus told His disciples to watch and pray that they

Sandro Botticelli shows an angel ministering to Jesus, whose agonized suffering in the garden has separated Him from His disciples, a separation symbolized by the fence. Meanwhile, the disciples sleep, lacking the stamina and will to remain awake in prayer with Jesus during His great trial.

might not enter into temptation. Jesus said that "the spirit indeed is willing, but the flesh is weak" (Mark 14:38; Matthew 26:41).

This would seem to indicate that the apostles stayed alert for a little while after Jesus awakened them, probably long enough to hear Him praying again. They must have questioned one another about what was happening with Jesus. Being tired, however, they would have talked for only a short while, perhaps only fifteen minutes, before returning to sleep. Presumably they were awake long enough to hear the prayer of Jesus recorded in Matthew's Gospel: "My Father, if this cannot pass unless I drink it, Your will be done" (26:42).

Jesus continued to pray for a period of time and returned once again to find the disciples asleep. This time both Matthew and Mark mention the heaviness of their eyes. This phrase may indicate the disciples were in a state of deep sleep, or REM sleep, which takes between forty-five and sixty minutes to attain. Jesus unsuccessfully attempts to awaken His disciples as a large crowd descends on the small band of men.

Based on the sleepiness of the disciples, Jesus was likely praying in the garden for approximately three hours. What did Jesus experience while praying? What caused so much agony that He sweat blood and needed an angel to support Him? As a family physician, I often have seen people suffering and near death. Some situations have made me cry as I have witnessed families and loved ones torn apart with grief and worry. I have watched patients and families suffer from tremendous anxiety, fear, and agony, and I have wondered how they cope with those burdens and continue their daily activities. However, I have never seen anyone in such agony that he experienced hemohidrosis (sweating blood). What did Jesus experience as He prayed? Certainly Jesus knew He was going to die. Four days before the Last Supper, Jesus had told the disciples that He was going to die, and He reiterated that fact earlier in the evening. What was unique about Jesus' agony in the Garden of Gethsemane?

The horror over which Jesus agonized was likely the mental anguish, and possibly even the experience of the physical trauma, related to His upcoming crucifixion. As the Son of God, Jesus knew His future. To have witnessed a crucifixion and know that you would soon experience the same torment would present a mental burden that indeed would require the support of an angel from God. It is comforting to know that Jesus asked His Father for help in His time of need. He has ascended on high to His Father and gives us His Spirit so that we can, like Him, ask our Father for help and aid when we are stressed and in need. Jesus' anguish in the garden allows us to identify with Him when we as human beings experience anguish. The responsibility of fulfilling the Father's will through His suffering and death in His humanity was a tremendous burden to bear. The acceptance of future punishment, torture, humiliation, and death gave Jesus the resolve to proceed.

Giovanni Guercino places the focus on Christ as the angel ministers to Him in the garden. The agony Jesus experiences is represented by the chalice He holds. This cup, which Christ has asked His Father to remove, represents the suffering our Savior will undergo on the wretched tree of death, the cross, and the blood that will flow from His veins into that cup.

Ephrem the Syrian expresses well Jesus' agony in the garden. Here the Author of life, fearful of death, prays for strength to drink from death's cup.

[Christ] knew what he was saying to his Father, and was well aware that this chalice could pass from him. . . . Just as he was hungry and thirsty, tired and had need of sleep, so too, he was afraid. . . . If he who is fearless was afraid [of death], and asked to be delivered from it, although he knew that it was impossible, how much more should others persevere in prayer before temptation, so that, in time of temptation, they may be delivered from it.

The Agony in the Garden

The New Testament Gospels attest that on the Mount of Olives in the Garden of Gethsemane Jesus underwent appalling mental agony. He declared to His disciples that His "soul was very sorrowful, even to death" (Matthew 26:38). Such deep distress can bring on a physical phenomenon called hemohidrosis, which causes sweat to appear to be the color of blood. St. Luke, probably a physician himself, gives an accurate clinical description of this rare phenomenon, which is thought to be provoked by great mental or emotional disturbance. St. Luke describes the struggle that occurs within the God-man, Jesus Christ. Jesus prays, "Father, not My will, but Yours, be done" (22:24), and He accepts His Father's will to be merciful to those who will deride and persecute Him. Yet Jesus' acceptance of His Father's will brings Him face-to-face with the suffering to come. St. Mark indicates that Jesus began to fear and to be heavy-hearted, no doubt a result of the impending suffering. Luke comments: "And being in an agony He prayed more earnestly; and His sweat became like great drops of blood falling down to the ground" (22:44). Luke's observation describes explicitly and clearly the process of sweating blood.

The physical process of hemohidrosis consists of a rupture (vasodilatation) of the blood vessels that supply the sweat glands (subcutaneous capillaries). The blood vessels become distended and burst when they come in contact with the millions of sweat glands distributed throughout the surface of the skin. Blood mingles with sweat, and it is this mixture that pearls over the whole surface of the body. Once this mixture of blood and sweat reaches the outside air, the blood coagulates, and these clots fall to the ground with profuse perspiration.

Giovanni Canavesio's painting evokes the extreme anguish Jesus suffers in the garden as He sweats drops of blood. As He envisions and experiences the foretaste of His Passion, Jesus' only recourse is to turn to His Father in prayer and complete trust.

These words of Martin Luther from a 1534 Holy Week sermon lead us to realize that Jesus underwent suffering unto death for our sake.

But why are you, O Lord Christ, so overcome with grief and terrified? Did you not say that you could petition your Father to send you more than twelve legions of angels—except that the Scripture must be fulfilled? If you are so terrified and afflicted by death, what hope is there for us poor, miserable people and sinners, if we are brought to the gallows or stake, or plague and other illness stare us in the face. We most certainly would despair, if death causes you so to tremble and shake. . . .

But it was for our sakes that this man, like no other person upon earth, was so afflicted; no one has ever been so terror-stricken by death as he was. When a man who has languished in jail for a long time is told, Get ready, you're going to be put to death, there's no alternative, he begins to agonize and fret, wrenching for a day, or three or four, his terror ever mounting, even more than when the hangman actually comes and executes him. That is to experience true death, when the incarcerated wretch gnaws away inwardly and the devil prompts the thought, You are mine and you must suffer. Then life takes on an entirely different aspect for the man; he speaks and acts differently. In short, his affliction is quite different from the plague or syphilis, for he experiences the anguish and throes of death, quite apart from bodily ailment or physical death.

It is in the nature of things for us human beings to find the struggles before death worse than death itself. When the devil has his way, despair reigns. The face of the individual involved in such struggle becomes tense, pale, and white, the eyes sunken and gloomy, the ears cold, and so on. But none of this compares with Christ our Lord's struggle in the Garden. Accordingly St. Luke states, "And being in agony he prayed more earnestly: and his sweat was as it were great drops of blood falling down to the ground." Christ went further than we; the heat and the fire he experienced pressed a bloody sweat from him.

On His soul lay the sins of the whole world. The death He had to suffer was a death caused by sin and imposed by the wrath of God. For since He had stepped into our place, had taken our sins upon Himself, and had ventured to render satisfaction for them, He felt both at once, the sins of the whole world and then the death He had to suffer for the sake of these sins. Therefore we are not only unable sufficiently to speak of this suffering and anguish, but we are also unable to think of it sufficiently.

All the anguish and fear of all other human beings are, by comparison, much, much too slight, because the sins of the whole world are resting on Him alone, and He is to pay for them with His death, whereas everyone of us has only his own sin resting on him. Yes, human suffering is slight when compared with that of this Man: all the world's sins—sins committed from the time of the first human being, Adam, until Judgment Day—burden the back of this one Man.

—Martin Luther

Hemohidrosis is so uncommon that it is rarely mentioned in medical literature. This often leads to doubt about the reality of the condition. Certainly the paucity of information about this phenomenon attests to its rarity. Yet St. Luke's description attests to its actual occurrence as he reports this phenomenon with astute qualities of observation and detail.

What medical evidence exists for hemohidrosis? Reportedly a sailor was so distraught at being caught in a fierce storm at sea that his face profusely sweated blood throughout the storm. Likewise, historical records mention a nun, surrounded by swords and daggers and in imminent danger of losing her life, who was so terrified and agitated that she discharged blood from every part of her body and died in the sight of her captors. King Charles IX of France reportedly suffered from an uncommon disease that caused him to bleed from all of his pores when he was near death. The element common to all these cases was extreme fear.

The intense perspiration documented by St. Luke also has been witnessed during crucifixions in camps for prisoners of war and during experiments on the process of crucifixion conducted by researchers. The intense diaphoresis, or profuse sweating, observed was remarkable because the air temperature was reportedly near freezing. Those who conducted these horrific experiments noted that the sweat stained the cement beneath the prisoners.

As in these historical cases, Jesus also sweated profusely, both during His agony as He prayed to His Father and as He hung on the cross. The evangelists describe this severe perspiration and the staining of Jesus' sweat, like blood, accurately and explicitly in the Gospels. This agony has been confirmed in other accounts of crucifixions. While He was praying in the Garden of Gethsemane, Jesus undoubtedly experienced something so emotionally and physically unsettling that He suffered hemohidrosis and felt it necessary to ask His Father for help.

In Jan Gossaert's *Agony in the Garden*, a young, clean-shaven Jesus is intent in His prayers. Apart from the moon, which itself is nearly cloaked, darkness hides everything—even the disciples are barely visible. The moonlight illumines Christ as the focal point even as He focuses on the host and chalice below the angel. Here is the Bread of God who gives life to the world (John 6:33). The angel comes to minister to the One who even now experiences the pouring out of His own blood into the cup of life for the world.

What did Jesus experience in the Garden of Gethsemane that caused His bloody sweat? It is likely that only what He was about to experience in His crucifixion could cause such anguish. Already in the garden, Jesus could have experienced the physical pain and suffering of His crucifixion, as well as the mental anguish. As the Son of God, Jesus not only could see His future but also could experience it. He could already have felt the whip on His body, the tearing of flesh from His bones. He could already have experienced the pain and suffering before it happened. Without question, crucifixion was vile, painful, cruel. Simply to think about it makes one cringe at what happens to the human body during this process. To feel the whipping and beating before it took place, to feel the weight of the crossbeam, to feel the nails driven through hands and feet, to endure the struggle to breathe before these events occurred—what anguish such foreknowledge would provoke. To be physically aware of all this before it happened would have been one of the most horrific experiences imaginable. Undoubtedly, the anguish Jesus experienced in the garden that night would have sufficiently stressed His human body, causing hemohidrosis.

If Jesus did experience the suffering of His crucifixion in the Garden of Gethsemane, then one can understand why He asked His Father to relieve Him of this terrible event. If Jesus knew, felt, and experienced His death already in the garden, thus asking His Father to spare Him, this reveals the monumental burden He endured for us.

With the help of His Father and support from an angel of heaven, who gave Him the resolve and strength to proceed, Christ completely accepted His forthcoming punishment, torture, humiliation, and death.

He clearly acknowledged that his "soul was sorrowful, even unto death," and his flesh weak. His intention was to show, from his troubled soul and weak flesh, that both his soul and body were fully human. For some have wrongly asserted that either the flesh or soul of Christ might be entirely different from ours. He sought by an extraordinary exhibition of the body-soul interaction, to show that neither body nor soul has any power at all of itself apart from the spirit. This is why he states first that the spirit is willing so that you may understand that you have within you the spirit's strength and not merely the weakness of the flesh. From this it is hoped that you may learn what to do under challenge, by what means to do it and how to order priorities. The weak must be brought under the strong—the flesh under the spirit. This will help you avoid making excuses, as you are now prone to do, for the weakness of your flesh while failing to understand the strength of the spirit.

—Tertullian

Jesus' eyes look imploringly toward His heavenly Father in this painting by Benvenuto di Giovanni. His prayer is answered with the blood of His suffering, death, and resurrection, which the angel bears. Thus we glimpse Jesus' complete reliance on His Father in these hours of great agony through the night.

You are a Christian. You carry the cross of Christ on your forehead. The mark stamped on you teaches you what you should profess. He was hanging on the cross, which you carry on your forehead. Do not delight in the sign of the wood but in the sign of the one hanging on it. When he was hanging on the cross, he was looking around at the people raving against him, putting up with their insults and praying for his enemies. While they were killing him, the doctor was curing the sick with his blood. He said, "Father, forgive them, because they do not know what they are doing." These words were not futile or without effect. Later, thousands of those people believed in the one they murdered, so that they learned how to suffer for him who had suffered for them and at their hands.

Brothers and sisters, we should understand this from the sign, from this stamp that Christians receive when they become catechumens. From this, we should understand why we are Christians.

—Augustine

This icon expresses the humanity of the merciful Son of God. The position of His body shows Jesus to be one who can suffer. Yet the iconographer has presented our Savior in such a way that even in His suffering He beckons us to come forward and receive the forgiveness found in His blood.

Hemohidrosis and severe diaphoresis (sweating) produces significant loss in bodily strength and resistance. These conditions would have intensified the pain of the beatings, the scourging, and the crucifixion that followed. After such an intense hemorrhage, the skin is swollen, extremely tender, and more sensitive to pain. In all likelihood, while Jesus prayed to His Father in the garden, His pain was physical, as well as emotional. When our Lord assumed His human body, He became able to experience pain, to suffer, and to die. With the assistance of the angel sent to Him from His Father, Jesus firmly resolved to endure these gruesome, painful experiences according to the Father's will. Jesus would not shirk from the blows or condemn those who delivered them. He would not accept the mild analgesic offered to cloud His mind. He would not drink, though every cell in His body would cry out for water. He accepted the Father's will and suffered the murderous rejection and unbelief—the sins—of all humanity in His crucified body. Christ Jesus, through His humanity, eventually succumbed to the evil and inhumane treatment meted out to Him. Yet before His death, He revealed once again that He was the Son of God, the faithful and divine Son of the Father, when He asked, "Father, forgive them, for they know not what they do" (Luke 23:34).

Often Christians dying of a terminal disease pray to Jesus. From their prayer emerges a beautiful spiritual resignation to accept their pathway through death to eternal rest in God. It is this acceptance of God's will that allows them to be ready for the final days of their lives and even to be hopeful for a blessed end and for their meeting with their heavenly Father at the resurrection. It is this same resolve that Jesus experienced when He asked His Father not to lead Him into this terrible ordeal. When He became spiritually resigned to the way in which the Father's will would be fulfilled, Jesus went with the soldiers willingly and peacefully. He did not permit any violence from His disciples, instructing them to put away their swords. He was reconciled to His Passion and looked forward to His reunion with His heavenly Father. Reflecting on Jesus' agony in the Garden of Gethsemane and learning about the cruelties inflicted on our Savior during the scourging and crucifixion only deepens our love for Him and our appreciation of what He suffered for us. His was truly an "experience of agony," the magnitude of which we hope never to experience.

Albrecht Dürer's engraving of the suffering in the garden shows a Christ whose heart is heavy and whose mind is extremely troubled. Jesus' face shows His agitation and agony, even as the disciples sleep.

The Suffering in the Garden

While praying in the garden that night, it is likely that Jesus not only foresaw but also experienced the events that would unfold over the next hours. In His agony, Jesus physically and emotionally experienced His crucifixion with all the pain, suffering, and destruction of His human body. He felt each stroke of the flagrum, its balls of metal tearing at His skin and muscles. He felt the weight of the crossbeam on His shoulders, as heavy as the weight of our sins on His soul. He felt the nails pierce through His wrists and feet. He felt His chest cavity being pulled apart and the panic of dying on the cross.

Experiencing these events before they actually happened was sufficiently horrific to cause Jesus' heart to be heavy and for His sweat to become like blood. The ultimate burden of being the anointed Son of God included not only visualizing but also experiencing the pain and agony of death before it occurred. Only the assistance of an angel could help Jesus as He suffered already the anguish of seeing His mother and feeling her pain on His way to Golgotha. Truly the heart-wrenching anguish and suffering Jesus experienced in the Garden of Gethsemane was sufficient to produce hemohidrosis. Visions of being punished, whipped, and crucified would be frightening, but to actually experience such suffering beforehand would be a horror impossible to imagine.

Christ's death on the cross and His victory over sin and death prepared early Christians to place themselves into God's hands as they faced persecution and martyrdom, often by the same means Christ was martyred—the cross. The words of Ignatius of Antioch reflect this great pastor's faith in Christ and His death, even in the face of his own horrific death. The Crucified One invites us to the same faith and hope.

Let no creature, visible or invisible, attract me, so that I may belong to Jesus Christ alone. Fire and the cross; herds of wild beasts; torn, stretched, rent, lacerated limbs; dislocated bones; crushed body; and all the tremendous torments of the devil let them all come upon me if only I can rest in Jesus Christ. All the kingdoms of this world and the joy of them are nothing to me. I prefer to die in Christ than to reign from one end of the earth to the other. I seek him who died for us; I long for him who rose again for our sakes.

In the depths of Jesus' suffering and in His willingness to suffer, Christians probe the very nature of God in His mercy and grace toward His human creatures. In a 1533 sermon for Good Friday, Martin Luther proclaimed:

And that is the paramount significance of the passion, that we realize and consider how Christ suffered in obedience to his heavenly Father and in our behalf to benefit us, that the Scripture might be fulfilled. . . . It is also well to consider the price paid for our sins, namely, that Christ did not pay gold or material goods, but rather his body and life, himself the offering for our sins . . . . At the same time one should bear in mind what great agony he suffered for us and how excruciating it was for him; how his sweat was as great drops of blood; how he was mocked, crowned with thorns, spit upon, scourged, nailed to the cross, and pierced for our sake. But this is the greatest and noblest consideration, that Christ had to suffer in order that he might fulfill the Scriptures.

We should diligently ponder all this, in order that we might not only recognize the greatness of the redemption, the price and the martyrdom, but also discern the love and good will toward us; how deeply concerned he is about us, and how his great heart, love, and compassion motivated him to give himself for us. That is why we should lovingly esteem both him who suffered such martyrdom for us and also the heavenly Father who ordained this and placed this martyrdom upon him. Such love should generate within us the realization of his goodwill toward us which prompted his voluntary martyrdom and suffering in our behalf. A human heart would need to be harder than stone, yes, harder than iron or steel not to be softened by this.

The events in the Garden of Gethsemane demonstrate the full and real humanity of Jesus. For more than thirty years, Jesus experienced all the joys, as well as the sorrows, of being a man. He knew the delight of being a son, a friend, and a mentor. As God, Jesus became fully man and accepted the burden of being the Suffering Servant, Immanuel—God with us in the flesh. This burden came to fulfillment when Jesus experienced beforehand, in all its fullness, the crucifixion. How reassuring to know that Jesus has suffered all that human beings possibly can suffer—and even more.

Jesus can sympathize with our weakness. Yet what is of the greatest consolation is that Jesus has been raised bodily from the dead, has conquered suffering and death, and suffers and dies no longer. This is the firm foundation of the Christian faith and the hope of all those baptized into Christ's death and resurrection.

Lucas Cranach the Elder placed himself between John the Baptist and Martin Luther in this richly detailed painting. A strong personal confession that forgiveness, life, and salvation are a gift of God through Jesus' shed blood, Cranach looks straight into the viewer's eyes as the blood of Christ pours directly on his head. Luther is pointing to 1 John 1:7 ("The blood of Jesus His Son cleanses us from all sin"), Hebrews 4:16 ("Let us then with confidence draw near to the throne of grace, that we may receive mercy and find grace to help in time of need"), and John 3:14 ("As Moses lifted up the serpent in the wilderness, so must the Son of Man be lifted up"). Beneath the cross, a lamb holds a banner with the words "The Lamb of God that takes away the sin of the world."

59

Although this painting by David Alfaro Siqueiros is of Christ's scourging, it depicts what Jesus would have foreseen, adding to His agonizing torment in the Garden of Gethsemane. With blood pouring from Him and engulfing Him, Jesus' confidence can be seen in His tightly gripped hands, which form a circle, an ancient symbol for the unity of God.

As the Son of God, Christ Jesus suffered physically and emotionally in the garden as He anticipated His impending crucifixion. Because He was able to know the future, Jesus could not deny what was to come. To prepare Himself, Jesus separated Himself from His followers to pray to His heavenly Father.

During the days preceding His crucifixion, and especially in His prayerful agony, Jesus experienced the same stages of emotion that the dying experience: denial and isolation, anger, bargaining, depression, and acceptance. In the days prior to His Passion, Jesus isolated Himself and His disciples from the activities of Jerusalem by residing in the neighboring town of Bethany. In the days prior to His death, a righteously angry and offended Jesus overturned the tables of the money changers in the temple. He showed frustration in the garden with His disciples when they could not stay awake with Him for even one hour. Always trusting in His Father, Jesus bargained with God to remove the burden of crucifixion from Him.

Jesus must have been saddened, even depressed, to tell His followers at the Last Supper that they would soon be without Him and would abandon Him, even Peter. Jesus shows dejection as He tells Judas to complete his intended task quickly. Disheartened, Jesus tries to wake His disciples for the last time and is resigned to let them continue sleeping. Jesus' final passage through the stages of grief was the acceptance of this path for the fulfillment of His Father's will.

Jesus told His disciples that He could ask His Father to summon more than twelve legions of angels to deliver Him. But Jesus told Peter to put away his sword. There would be no angelic deliverers, because all who would take up the sword ultimately perish by the sword. The mercy of God—the will of God—was Jesus' desire, not deliverance for Himself. There was to be no more violence. So Jesus' last miracle that night was to heal the severed ear of one of His captors. Complete acceptance: His hour was at hand!

As you pray, recognize that as Christ fulfilled His Father's will, the Father's will for you is accomplished. You belong to God's holy people!

It is truly good, right, and salutary that we should at all times and in all places give thanks to You, holy Lord, almighty Father, everlasting God, through Jesus Christ, our Lord, who, having created all things, took on human flesh and was born of the virgin Mary. For our sake He died on the cross and rose from the dead to put an end to death, thus fulfilling Your will and gaining for You a holy people. Therefore with angels and archangels and with all the company of heaven we laud and magnify Your glorious name, evermore praising You.

Chapter Three

THe Suffering of Jesus Christ

From the Arrest to the Crucifixion at Golgotha

Your soul in griefs unbounded,
Your head with thorns surrounded,
You died to ransom me.
The cross for me enduring,
The crown for me securing,
You healed my wounds
*   and set me free.*

Guercino depicts the betrayal of Christ with power and pathos. The faces of the participants reveal their thoughts and words. Carrying out the temple priests' will, the men seize Jesus with violence. Feeling guilty, Judas clutches his moneybag and shrinks from Jesus' disappointment, moving away from the light emanating from Christ. The soldiers pull and grab at Jesus, who seems calm and at peace, the epitome of trust in His Father.

The Trials of Jesus

Jesus' hour was at hand, the hour of His deliverance into the hands of sinners, sin, death, and, to all appearances, the power of the devil. Jesus' betrayal and deliverance into the clutches of the kingdom of evil was manifested in His arrest, trial, scourging, and bearing of the cross. Here the Son of God was truly seen as the Son of Man, whose servanthood to His Father and to humanity in suffering shows the very heart and nature of God. In Jesus, the Suffering Servant, humanity finds God most deeply embedded in the flesh to restore humanity to God's life for His creatures.

Following His arrest in the Garden of Gethsemane, Jesus was taken before the Jewish Sanhedrin and accused of crimes against Jewish law. According to Scripture and Jewish historians, during His trials before the Sanhedrin and while being marched to the Roman authorities, Jesus was beaten on the head and lashed with reeds, though Jesus' skin probably was swollen and sensitive from the hemo-hidrosis. And during His trials, the Sanhedrin's police and Pilate's and Herod's guards blindfolded Jesus, hit Him on the head and in the face, and spat on Him.

The very heart of God toward His creatures is enfleshed in the incarnation of His Son and extended to His creatures through Jesus' death and resurrection. Through this prayer, fix your eyes on God's heart in Jesus.

Merciful and everlasting God, You did not spare Your only Son but delivered Him up for us all to bear our sins on the cross. Grant that our hearts may be so fixed with steadfast faith in Him that we fear not the power of sin, death, and the devil; through the same Jesus Christ, our Lord, who lives and reigns with You and the Holy Spirit, one God, now and forever. Amen.

The facial images on the Shroud of Turin portray a man with significant swelling around his right eye and with broken cartilage in his nose. Jesus was ridiculed and manhandled by His captors throughout the processions from each place of examination and trial.

Unable to gather enough evidence to convincingly condemn Jesus, and incapable of rendering the death

Jesus' deliverance into the hands of sinful men marks the final act in the coming of God's kingdom among us. In the words of this English carol, it is the beginning of Jesus' day of dancing and our invitation to join His dance.

Sing O my love,
O my love, my love, my love;
This have I done for my true love.

Tomorrow shall be my dancing day:
I would my true love did so chance
To see the legend of my play,
To call my true love to my dance.

For thirty pence Judas me sold,
His covetousness for to advance;
"Mark whom I kiss,
*   the same do hold,*
The same is he shall lead
*   the dance."*

Then on the cross hanged I was,
Where a spear to my heart
*   did glance;*
There issued forth both water
*   and blood,*
To call my true love to my dance.

Then down to hell I took my way,
For my true love's deliverance,
And rose again on the third day,
Up to my true love
*   and to the dance.*

Jesus suffered in humiliating ways at the hands of the guards of the Sanhedrin, as well as the soldiers of Pilate and Herod. In this woodcut by Albrecht Dürer, Jesus' face is hidden. Isaiah tells us that in a surge of anger, God hides His face from sinful mankind (Isaiah 54:8).

penalty without Roman approval, the Sanhedrin took Jesus to the Fortress of Antonia for a trial before the Roman hierarchy in the guise of Pontius Pilate, the Roman governor. The Jewish elders were convinced they could try Jesus as a man who threatened to undermine Roman authority by claiming to be the Jewish Messiah. This was the equivalent of treason, a capital crime punishable by death.

These drawings by Albrecht Dürer show Jesus bound, pulled, beaten, forced to the ground, blindfolded, spit on, mocked, and derided. In the words of Isaiah, "He was despised, and we esteemed Him not" (Isaiah 53:3).

Christ, the life of all the living,
Christ, the death of death, our foe,
Who, Thyself for me once giving
To the darkest depths of woe:
Through Thy suff'rings, death,
    and merit
I eternal life inherit.
Thousand, thousand thanks shall be,
Dearest Jesus, unto Thee.

Thou, ah! Thou, hast taken
    on Thee
Bonds and stripes, a cruel rod;
Pain and scorn were heaped
    upon Thee,
O Thou sinless Son of God!
Thus didst Thou my soul deliver
From the bonds of sin forever.
Thousand, thousand thanks shall be,
Dearest Jesus, unto Thee.

Thou hast borne the smiting only
That my wounds might all be whole;
Thou hast suffered, sad and lonely,
Rest to give my weary soul;
Yea, the curse of God enduring,

Blessing unto me securing.
Thousand, thousand thanks shall be,
Dearest Jesus, unto Thee.

Heartless scoffers did surround Thee,
Treating Thee with shameful scorn
And with piercing thorns they
    crowned Thee.
All disgrace Thou, Lord, hast borne,
That as Thine Thou mightest
    own me
And with heav'nly glory crown me.
Thousand, thousand thanks shall be,
Dearest Jesus, unto Thee.

Thou hast suffered men to
    bruise Thee,
That from pain I might be free;
Falsely did Thy foes accuse Thee:
Thence I gain security;
Comfortless Thy soul did languish
Me to comfort in my anguish.
Thousand, thousand thanks shall be,
Dearest Jesus, unto Thee.

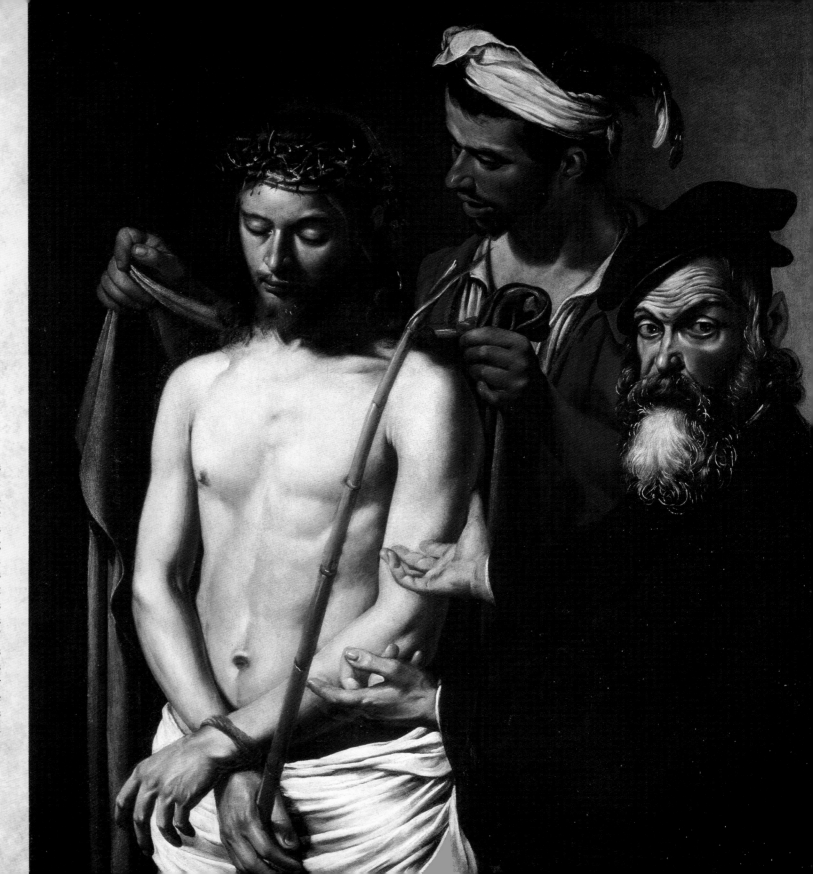

Notice the contrast in this painting by Caravaggio. The Sanhedrin claimed Jesus was a subversive revolutionary, yet He is shown meekly accepting the mockery of the crown and robe. Jesus appears as a very young man, almost childlike innocence is His robe, recalling that His first title was "the Child." As Pilate presents Jesus to the people, seeking His release, the crowds call for His death—the ultimate injustice that will bring us forgiveness and eternal life.

The Jewish leaders hoped that Pontius Pilate would put Jesus to death with little fanfare. However, Pilate had a great deal to gain if Jesus could oust the Jewish Sanhedrin. Although a cruel man, Pilate appears kindly disposed to Jesus, probably because of His potential to disrupt Jewish tradition. Pilate was in no hurry to put this man to death and tried several times to spare Jesus.

The Sanhedrin could not produce credible witnesses to prove that Jesus encouraged the people to revolt against Rome, so Pilate repeatedly proclaimed to the Jewish leaders that Jesus was innocent. Not to be denied, the Sanhedrin announced that Jesus claimed to be the Son of God, and according to Jewish law, this blasphemous claim meant Jesus must die. Again Pilate refused to put Jesus to death. In fact, Pilate did all he could to release this man whose innocence was obvious to all and whose actions and behavior commanded respect. Finally, the Sanhedrin announced that Jesus had declared Himself a king. The Jewish leaders accused Pilate of not being a friend of Caesar if Jesus was released. As a territorial ruler, such a threat struck at Pilate's Achilles' heel. If these claims reached Rome and Pilate had failed to address the threat, the Roman emperor might take disciplinary action, threatening Pilate's political career and even his life.

As a result, the Sanhedrin achieved its goal, and Pilate was forced to treat this man who claimed to be a king as a Roman subversive. Condemnation was a forgone conclusion. The law called for crucifixion.

Before handing Jesus over to the Sanhedrin, Pilate visibly expressed his reluctance concerning the death sentence. To absolve himself of guilt related to putting this innocent man to death, Pilate ceremonially washed his hands of the affair and declared himself innocent of shedding an innocent man's blood.

The Evangelists, Matthew, Mark, and Luke, tell how men spit upon and slandered the Lord in the high priest's home. Who can repeat all these blasphemies? This blasphemous maltreatment went on continuously through the night until morning. The Evangelists touch on this just briefly, telling how they covered up his face and struck him in the face with their fists, toying with him, saying,

"Prophesy, Christ, who is it that smote thee?" . . .

Just as Christ of his own free will gladly became weak for our sakes, and allowed himself to be taken captive and bound, so also for our sake, of his own free will and gladly, he allows himself to be accused, mocked, spit upon, sentenced, condemned, and killed as a sinner, even though he was not guilty of death. . . .

We Christians exult in this, that Christ, true God and man, suffered of his own will gladly. He did not wish to exercise His might, and his adversaries were not able to prove him guilty. What he did, he did for our sakes, so that he might break the stranglehold which sin, death, and the devil had on us.

—Martin Luther

A dread and marvelous mystery we see come to pass this day. He whom none may touch is seized; He who looses Adam from the curse is bound. He who tries our hearts and inner thoughts is unjustly brought to trial. He who closed the abyss is shut in prison. He before whom the powers of heaven stand with trembling hands, stands before Pilate; the Creator is struck by the hand of a creature. He who comes to judge the living and the dead is condemned to the cross; the Destroyer of hell is enclosed in a tomb.

Then Pilate took the last jab at the manipulative Sanhedrin by writing the *titulus*, or inscription, for the cross in Hebrew, Latin, and Greek for all to read. By means of the inscription placed at the top of the crossbeam, Pilate announced the crime that brought about Jesus' crucifixion: that "Jesus of Nazareth" was the "King of the Jews." Along with Jesus' scourging, His procession through the streets, and His crucifixion, Pilate reminded the Jewish people of their subjection to the Roman Empire. By sentencing the Jewish king to the vulgar and dehumanizing act of crucifixion, the Romans were laughing in the face of the Jews and proclaiming the supposed powerlessness of their God.

Pilate epitomizes all humans when he washes his hands of responsibility for Jesus' death. While he had the power to release Jesus, Pilate chose not to do so. Instead, he justifies himself and takes no responsibility. Pilate blames someone else for the death of the innocent Son of God. In this engraving, Albrecht Dürer couples Pilate's claim of innocence with the leading away of the Innocent One to the way of the cross.

It was providential and the fruit of God's inexpressible purpose that the title was written in three languages: one in Hebrew, another in Latin and another in Greek. For it lay in plain view, proclaiming the kingdom of our Savior Christ in the most widely known of all languages . . . fulfilling the prophecy that had been spoken concerning him. For the wise Daniel said that there was given him glory and a kingdom and that all nations and languages shall serve him. Similarly the holy Paul teaches us, crying out that "every knee shall bow; of things in heaven and things on earth and things under the earth. And every tongue shall confess that Jesus Christ is Lord, to the glory of God the Father." Therefore the title proclaiming Jesus "king" was, as it were, the true firstfruits of the confession of tongues.

—Cyril of Alexandria

Perhaps it is good that Hieronymus Bosch's painting does not depict the soldiers with evil demeanors. Thus we see these men as not too different from ourselves. As He prepares to receive the crown of thorns, Christ is calm and serene. His serenity contrasts with the evil of which humans are capable, a capacity for evil proved by the fact that the Son of God suffers at the hands of those who, like us, deride Him.

With Johann Sebastian Bach, ponder the good that comes to you from Jesus' thorn-pierced brow. Ponder, my soul, with anxious pleasure, with bitter delight and half-uneasy heart, in Jesus' agony your highest good; how, for you, out of the thorns that pierce him, the key-of-heaven flowers blossom! You can break off much sweet fruit from his wormwood, so behold him without ceasing!

The Roman soldiers reveled in the chance to humiliate the Jews. As professional soldiers in a superbly accomplished and decorated army, these men had no sympathy for non-Romans, especially non-Roman criminals. Their hatred of the Jews was intensified during the Feast of Passover because they were constantly confronted with the crowds of Jews gathered for the religious festival. Roman soldiers and executioners were given complete liberty to mock and taunt victims condemned to death. In this way, the Romans ruled by intimidation and cruelty. So the soldiers given charge over Jesus took every opportunity to mock the Jews and their newly declared king.

The soldiers placed a crown or caplike bundle of bush limbs with thorns on Jesus' head. The limbs may have come from a tree commonly used for fires in Judea—the *Ziziphus spina-christi*, a kind of small lotus tree. The branches of this tree feature long, sharp thorns. Branches could have been quickly bent together to form a caplike structure that conformed to Jesus' head. The headband of thorns seen in artwork today did not become a popular interpretation of the crown of thorns until the fifteenth century. The Shroud of Turin shows more than seventy head wounds that might be typical of such a caplike structure. These head wounds apparently continued bleeding even after Jesus died.

The extrabiblical legend of St. Veronica tells of a pagan woman who took pity on Christ and used her cloth to wipe His face as He carried the cross to Golgotha. Thus the image of Jesus' face was transferred to the cloth. With a single, continuous line that starts in the middle of Jesus' nose and spirals out to the edge of the page, Claude Mellan depicts the image of the suffering Christ (detail of *The Sudarium of Saint Veronica*). Imagine Jesus looking at you in pain, yet with mercy, much like it is imagined He looked at Veronica.

The Lord's crown of thorns prophetically pointed to us who once were barren but are placed around him through the church of which he is the head. But it is also a type of faith, of life in respect to the substance of the wood, of joy in respect to the appellation of crown, of danger in respect to the thorn. For there is no approaching the Word without blood. . . . They crowned Jesus raised up high, testifying to their own ignorance. . . . This crown is the flower of those who have believed on the glorified One, but it covers with blood and chastises those who have not believed. It is a symbol, too, of the Lord's successful work, he having borne on his head (the princely part of his body) all our iniquities by which we were pierced. For he by his own passion rescued us from offenses and sins and other thorns. And having destroyed the devil, deservedly said in triumph, "O Death, where is your sting?"

—*Clement of Alexandria*

In this engraving, Albrecht Dürer emphasizes the mockery of the soldiers. They have seated Christ on a "throne," crowned Him with thorns, clothed Him in a robe, and given Him a reed to hold. He appears resigned to their abuse, recalling Isaiah's prophecy, "He will not cry aloud or lift up His voice . . . He will faithfully bring forth justice" (Isaiah 42:2–3).

The soldiers intensified the mockery of Jesus by placing a purple or red robe, symbolic of royalty, over His back. He was given a reed or stick as His scepter. Once again, the soldiers hit Jesus in the face repeatedly, spat on Him, and hit His head with the mock scepter. The repetitive trauma to His head, which was covered with thorns, contributed to a continuous loss of blood, progressive weakness, and diminished physical resistance. Approximately 25 percent of the heart's cardiac output flows to the head. With the ongoing abuse and the crown of thorns causing continuous loss of blood, Jesus would have slipped gradually into a state of circulatory shock and profound weakness.

During the night, amid the trials and the physical punishment Jesus endured while being mocked, a strong and vibrant man was robbed of much of His strength. Yet Jesus' condition at the end of the trials shows that He had been healthy prior to the arrest. Amazingly, Jesus did not pass out from the loss of body fluid (hypovolemia) or from shock as a result of the trauma. While Jesus was in good physical condition, He already had suffered great emotional stress in Gethsemane and physical punishment during His trials. He had been kept awake all night and forced to walk approximately two and a half miles from the trial before the Sanhedrin, to Pilate, to Herod, and then back to Pilate. Stress and fatigue, hemohidrosis and its associated dehydration and bleeding, and the head and facial beatings and blood loss from the crown of thorns had taken a significant toll on Jesus' body. Although Jesus was now severely weakened, He was firmly committed to His Father's will, a commitment developed and confirmed during His time of agony and prayer in the Garden of Gethsemane. Jesus would now face the terrifying ordeal of scourging, an ordeal He had already experienced in the garden.

The soldiers' mockery of Christ exemplifies the mercy of God toward those who rage against Him with weapons of spirit, mind, and soul. In the words of Icelandic poet Hallgrimur Petursson, Jesus takes our mockery of Him and in turn exalts those who mock Him.

The soldiers led the Savior out,
Their band together calling
Into the hall with cruel shout;
In blasphemy appalling
They stripped Him of His
   clothes, and spread
A purple robe about Him—red
Beneath it blood was falling.
Of thorns they platted swift
   a crown,

With points for sharpest
   paining;
Hard on His head
   they crushed it down,
Until the blood drops raining
Gushed forth,
His sacred eyes and face,
Which ever looked upon
   our race
In love, with crimson staining.
As scepter in His hand a reed
They placed with hate unfeeling;
They hailed Him kin, and
   mocked His need,
In scorn before Him kneeling:
And as they spat and smote
   Him sore, their laughter
   louder than before,

Through all the hall
   went pealing.
By Thy abasement, Lord, I gain
My royal exaltation;
Eternal honour I attain
Through Thy humiliation;
Amid the ransomed hosts I take,
For my adored Redeemer's sake,
With joy my blood-bought
   station.
And so, while life shall last,
   Thy grace I would be ever
   praising,
To Thy dear name in every place
My thankful song upraising;
In everything Thy blessed will
   I would with ready heart
   fulfill,
And tell Thy love amazing.

The Scourging

Do we fully understand what happened to Jesus during His scourging? How extreme were the beatings that destroyed Jesus' healthy and vibrant thirty-three-year-old body, leading to death in a short time on the cross? What did Jesus experience at the hands of the Roman guard? Was it more than just a whipping with a strap? Was it enough to cause Jesus to die more rapidly than expected? Scourging (a severe form of whipping) was a standard procedure before all forms of capital punishment, regardless of the method of execution—hanging, beheading, burning at the stake, or crucifixion. Scourging was intended to physically punish and weaken the victim. The destruction of skin and muscle produced severe pain and continuous blood loss.

Rich with symbolism, Lorenzo Monaco's painting depicts the glorified Christ rising from His tomb, which is positioned before the cross of death. He embraces Mary and allows John to touch Him that he may believe. At the front of the tomb is a chalice, a symbol of the Lord's Supper, in which is given Christ's blood poured out on the cross. Medieval belief held that the pelican pierced her breast to feed her young with her blood, even as Christ does for His children on the cross and in the Lord's Supper. Thus the pelican and her brood above the cross are symbolic of Christ's sacrifice. To the right above the crossbeam, Judas betrays with a kiss, and Peter and the woman to the left evoke Peter's denial of Christ. The *Arma Christi*, or instruments of the Passion, surround Jesus: the money for the betrayal; Peter's sword; a torch; many hands of torture; the blindfold; the rod, pillar, and whips of His scourging; the pitcher and basin Pilate used to wash his hands; the hammer and nails; the cross; the stick and sponge to quench Jesus' thirst; the spear that pierced His side; and the ladder and cloak used to remove Jesus' body from the cross. In one painting, the sweeping drama of Jesus' suffering is brought to remembrance. Here is the One "whom God put forward as a propitiation by His blood, to be received by faith" (Romans 3:25).

This depiction of Christ's scourging emphasizes that He suffered this punishment for us. Diego Rodriguez de Silva y Velasquez shows Christ turning toward the believing soul, depicted here as the worshiping child, who kneels in trust beside Him. The weapons of the scourging lie between this faithful soul and the tortured Christ. We are not to heed the rebuke of the disciples, but instead follow the angel who leads the the believing soul to Jesus, "for to such belongs the kingdom of heaven" (Matthew 19:14). Indeed, we must all become like little children (Matthew 18:3) before the suffering Christ.

As the imagery of this early Christian prayer recalls Jesus' Passion, especially the scourging, we are reminded of the benefits we receive from Christ's suffering, including love, forgiveness, and eternal life.

For us you have drunk gall to take from us all bitterness; you have drunk a bitter wine for us to lift us from our weariness; you have been despised for us, that the dew of immortality might be poured upon us; you have been beaten with scourges to ensure to our frailty eternal life; you have been crowned with thorns that your faithful might be crowned with the evergreen laurels of love; you have been wrapped in a winding sheet that we might be clothed in your strength; you were laid in the tomb that in a new age loving kindness might again be granted to us.

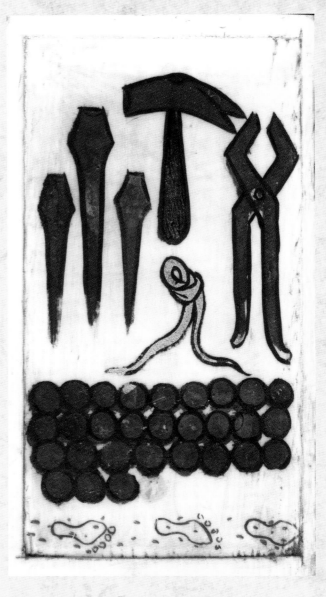

These images of the tools of Christ's torture are part of a fourteenth-century German devotional booklet. It features scenes of the Passion and encourages meditation on Christ's suffering and death. The images and texts encourage the reader to enter personally into each scene and to realize that our Savior accepted these sufferings not from only one individual, but from all of us.

The first eight panels depict scenes from the Passion, the last four, which are the *Arma Christi*, are shown here. The series concludes with scenes of the resurrection and the image of Christ.

The *Arma Christi* include items used during Christ's Passion as well as symbols of the episodes of the Passion narrative. The hand symbolizes

the times Christ was slapped, especially in His trial before the Sanhedrin. The red oblong shape represents the wound in Christ's side. The nails and hammer used to fasten Christ to the cross are shown with the pincers used to remove the nails. The blindfold and the thirty pieces of silver paid to Judas for the betrayal recall Christ's arrest and trials. The bloody footprints bring to mind Christ's

The Roman officer (centurion) in charge of the crucifixion detail also was responsible for the scourging. Specifically, he would ensure the victim did not die prematurely because the scourging was not intended to cause death. The criminal was to die on the cross. The severity of the scourging was inversely related to the length of time it took the victim to die on the cross. In other words, if the victim was not whipped very badly, he would hang on the cross for a longer period of time. If he was beaten severely and suffered a great deal of blood loss, punctured lungs, ruptured kidneys, bleeding beneath the skull, or other complications of trauma, then he would die quickly on the cross. Since the death of Jesus occurred more quickly than expected, He must have been scourged severely.

The instrument generally used by the Romans to whip victims was a *flagrum*, a device designed to cause severe pain and to destroy the body. The flagrum had a short, wooden handle from which extended wrapped leather thongs two to three feet in length. Sharp sheep bones and metal balls were attached to the ends of the leather thongs. The metal balls peppered the skin with welts. Then the animal bones would dig into the welts and rip open the skin. Subsequent lashes would expose muscle and even pull it out in shreds. Each lash of the whip produced excruciating and ongoing pain. Continuous blood loss induced a state of early shock. Scourging also traumatized the lungs and kidneys and would lead to progressive dehydration, blood loss, and severe weakness.

You belong to Christ for you have been enrolled in the books of life. There the blood of the Lord serves for your purple robe, and your broad stripe is his own cross.

—*Tertullian*

procession to Golgotha. The dice illustrated on the tunic represent the soldiers who gambled for Christ's cloak. The reed and the whip were part of Christ's scourging and mocking at the hands of the soldiers. The spear pierced Christ's side to ascertain His death, while the ladder was necessary to remove His body from the cross. The green rectangle represents Christ's garden tomb.

The victim to be scourged was generally naked, his arms tied above his head as he stood facing a large pillar. Jesus' back, neck, buttocks, and legs were whipped repeatedly. As an indicator of the kind of scourging Jesus endured, two soldiers most likely carried out the scourging of the individual wrapped in the Shroud of Turin. On the shroud's image, the lashes spread out in two fan shapes across the back, buttocks, and legs. The markings covering the entire buttock region indicate that the victim was naked during the scourging. There are more than one hundred and twenty marks across the victim's back in groupings of two's or three's. The straps lashed against the back, and then wrapped around the front, causing pain throughout the entire body. The only areas not covered with strap and ball marks are the forearms, which were suspended upward to hold the victim in place against the pillar. Only those blows leaving marks (contusions) or tears (excoriations) would have been impressed on the cloth that covered Jesus' body after it was removed from the cross. And areas of the skin lashed repeatedly would not have shown how many times they were hit. The number of lashes Jesus received was undoubtedly greater than the one hundred and twenty marks that appear on the victim impressed on the Shroud of Turin.

In his St. John Passion, *Johann Sebastian Bach celebrates the victory that is ours because Christ endured the scourging.*

Consider, how His blood-tinged back, in all aspects is just like the sky. Thereon, after the floodwaves of our sins' deluge have passed by, the most beautiful rainbow remains as a sign of God's grace!

Albrecht Dürer's sketch emphasizes the humiliation of Christ as, standing nearly naked, He endures the soldiers' whips. Clothed in flesh at creation, Adam donned clothes in embarassment and humiliation before the Creator. Here the new Adam is stripped naked that by His suffering and resurrection, the beauty of human flesh might be made whole. Contrasted with the determination of the soldiers, Christ appears steeled for what He must endure.

This reflection by the theologian Romanus Melodus shows the servanthood of Christ on our behalf: the One who was the pillar of Israel is tied in all humility to a pillar. In that humiliating act, the pillar of our salvation in the Church is carved forever.

Like a lion they roared to seize the life of the lamb, Christ. Pilate fulfilled their will, flogged Thee, the gentle One. So he set to work on Thy back. . . . The Redeemer endured the lash; the Deliverer was in chains; Nude and stretched out on a pillar, Is He who in a pillar of cloud formerly spoke to Moses and Aaron. He who established the pillars of the earth, as David said [Psalm 75:3], is fastened to a pillar. He who showed the people the road in the desert, (For the pillar of fire appeared before them), He has been attached to a pillar; The rock is on a column and the church is hewn in stone for me.

Jesus was scourged unjustly so that he might deliver us from the punishment we deserved. He was beaten and struck so that we might beat Satan, who had beaten us, and that we might escape from the sin that cleaves to us through the original transgression. For if we think correctly, we shall believe that all of Christ's sufferings were for us and on our behalf and that they have power to release us and deliver us from all those calamities we have deserved because of our rebellion against God.

—*Cyril of Alexandria*

In this painting attributed to Caravaggio, Christ is being tied to the pillar in preparation for the scourging. We see the agony on our Savior's face, the business-like determination of the soldiers, and the humiliation Christ underwent for us. Yet the light shines on His body and His face is not hidden from us. Even the sin of wicked men must succumb to Christ's brightness. "I am the light of the world," Jesus says, "whoever follows Me will not walk in darkness, but will have the light of life" (John 8:12).

We know from analysis of the terminology used to describe Jesus' scourging that He was "severely whipped." Jewish law limited the number of lashes used to weaken a victim to forty. To avoid a miscount, the lashes often were limited to thirty-nine. However, the Romans had no such restrictions, and it appears the Jewish limit was greatly exceeded in Jesus' case. Officially, Jesus was being crucified because of the threat His messianic claims posed to the Roman Empire. He was being scourged by Roman soldiers who had no great admiration for the Jewish people at the same time that Jerusalem was swelling to more than three hundred thousand people, primarily of Jewish origin. In the context of a hostile religious and political environment, most likely the innermost hatred of the Romans was unleashed on this Jewish man, Jesus Christ. He would be an extreme example of the Roman control of and contempt for the race and religion of the Jews.

I said, In the middle of my days
  I must depart;

I am consigned to the gates of Sheol
  for the rest of my years.

I said, I shall not see the LORD,
  the LORD in the land of the living;

I shall look on man no more
  among the inhabitants of the world.

My dwelling is plucked up and removed from me
  like a shepherd's tent;
  like a weaver I have rolled up my life;

He cuts me off from the loom;
  from day to night You bring me to an end;
  I calmed myself until morning;

like a lion He breaks all my bones;
  from day to night You bring me to an end.

Like a swallow or a crane I chirp;
  I moan like a dove.

My eyes are weary with looking upward.
  O LORD, I am oppressed;
  be my pledge of safety!

What shall I say? For He has spoken to me,
  and He Himself has done it.

I walk slowly all my years
  because of the bitterness of my soul.

O Lord, by these things men live,
  and in all these is the life of my spirit.
  Oh restore me to health and make me live!

Behold, it was for my welfare
  that I had great bitterness;

but in love You have delivered my life
  from the pit of destruction,

for You have cast all my sins
  behind Your back.

For Sheol does not thank You;
  death does not praise You;

those who go down to the pit do not hope
  for Your faithfulness.

The living, the living, he thanks You,
  as I do this day;

the father makes known to the children
  Your faithfulness.

The LORD will save me,
  and we will play my music on stringed instruments

all the days of our lives,
  at the house of the LORD.
                Isaiah 38:10–20

Is it possible to fully understand what happened to Jesus during His scourging? What did He experience at the hands of the Roman guard? Was His beating more severe than usual, severe enough to hasten His death on the cross? How much pain did Jesus endure as the sacrifice for human sin? Try to put yourself in Jesus' place. Reflect upon the feel of the lash as it reaches across your back and wraps around the front of your body over and over again. Think about the metal balls as they hit your skin. Feel the welts form, then rip away from your body as the sharp bone fragments strike. This intense, repetitive pain would have continued for what seemed like an eternity, the only thing keeping you conscious. Jesus already had undergone intense agony in the Garden of Gethsemane. His skin was swollen and sensitive from the hemohidrosis. Then the metal balls and pieces of sharp bone struck His body. Know in your heart that Jesus truly suffered in your place.

As indicated earlier, the severity of the beatings hastened the victim's death on the cross. A person's death from crucifixion was expected to take from three hours to three days. Pontius Pilate was surprised that Jesus died in about three hours. By the end of His scourging, Jesus surely was in a critical physical state. Deprived of food, water, and sleep, He had undergone emotional trauma and hemohidrosis (sweating blood) in the garden. He had repeatedly been struck in the face and on the head, and a crown of thorns had been driven into His scalp. His severe scourging brought blood loss, body fluid loss, kidney and lung trauma, and excruciating and unrelenting pain. By the time the soldiers finished, Jesus was irreparably broken. Most likely He would have died shortly thereafter, even if He had not been crucified. The Roman soldiers had performed their job well. After His scourging, a robe was draped over Jesus' shoulders, and He was given a crude staff as a scepter.

Quentin Massys has painted Christ as an emaciated, wasted, and abandoned figure, truly the Man of Sorrows. Pilate stands to the left, presenting Jesus to those seeking His crucifixion. Pilate's posture with hands upraised implies he will intervene no more. Pilate's resignation contrasts with the emotions of the man binding Jesus. His face captures the anger, jealousy, and spite of all who persecuted Christ and summarizes the words of Caiaphas, the high priest, "that it is better for you that one man should die for the people, not that the whole nation should perish" (John 11:50). The man's face proclaims, "Behold the man!"

Jesus is looking at you, pleading with you, suffering for you that you might belong to Him. In His arms, He bears the tools that inflicted His scourging, tools by which He has suffered to claim you as His own.

The robe, the crown of thorns, and the reed mocked Jesus' messianic claims to be the King of Israel. Again, He was hit in the face, spat on, and clubbed with His staff repeatedly. Jesus suffered a great deal of pain and major blood loss by the time He was led to the site of His crucifixion. As Dr. Edwards so appropriately points out: "The severe scourging, with its intense pain and appreciable blood loss, most probably left Jesus in a pre-shock state. Moreover, hemohidrosis had rendered His skin particularly tender. The physical and mental abuse meted out by the Jews and the Romans, as well as the lack of food, water, and sleep, also contributed to His generally weakened state."

Imagine a hat of large pointed thorns thrust on your head. Now someone hits that hat repeatedly with a stick. Think about the last time you were cut on your head; remember the pain and how much it bled. Jesus wore this crown of suffering for you.

At this point before His crucifixion, Jesus' physical condition was so destroyed that even if He would have been transported to one of the finest modern emergency rooms, it is highly unlikely that He would have survived.

Bearing the Cross

As was the custom, Jesus was forced to carry His own cross following the terrible ordeal of scourging. The events that occurred during the procession to His place of crucifixion often are referred to as "The Way of the Cross."

On this journey through Jerusalem, the Gospels indicate that Jesus required assistance in carrying His cross. He also encountered Jewish women who were wailing for Him. Although the Gospels do not reveal details about Jesus' condition during the procession, it is possible that He fell repeatedly, had His face wiped clean, and experienced an emotional encounter with His mother, Mary. He was subjected yet again to public humiliation and embarrassment on His way to Golgotha.

Behold, the LORD has proclaimed
to the end of the earth:

Say to the daughter of Zion,
"Behold, your salvation comes;

behold, His reward is with Him,
and His recompense before Him."

And they shall be called The Holy People,
The Redeemed of the LORD;

and you shall be called Sought Out,
A City Not Forsaken.

Who is this who comes from Edom,
in crimsoned garments from Bozrah,

He who is splendid in His apparel,
marching in the greatness
of His strength?

"It is I, speaking in righteousness,
mighty to save."

Why is Your apparel red,
and Your garments like his who
treads in the winepress?

"I have trodden the winepress alone,
and from the peoples no one
was with Me;

I trod them in My anger
and trampled them in My wrath;

their lifeblood spattered on My garments,
and stained all My apparel.

For the day of vengeance was in My heart,
and My year of redemption had come.

I looked, but there was no one to help;
I was appalled, but there was no one
to uphold;

so My own arm brought Me salvation,
and My wrath upheld Me.

I trampled down the peoples in My anger;
I made them drunk in My wrath,
and I poured out their lifeblood
on the earth."

I will recount the steadfast love
of the LORD,
the praises of the LORD,

according to all that the LORD
has granted us,
and the great goodness to the house
of Israel

that He has granted them according
to His compassion,
according to the abundance
of His steadfast love.

Isaiah 62:11–63:7

As Christ bears His cross to Golgotha, the women follow, wailing. Benvenuto di Giovanni captures the depth of Jesus' sorrow, pain, and weakness. Our Savior's countenance contrasts with the evil and sin etched on the faces of those cajoling Him to complete the path to the place of crucifixion. Imagine this is your city, your society, your culture. Christ Jesus came into the world to save sinners of every age, tribe, nationality, and language.

87

Jacopo Bassano depicts all those following Jesus as plunging to the ground with Him as He falls under the weight of the cross. Only Mary remains standing, perhaps strengthened by the Word of God in her heart. Rather than burdened, Bassano painted Jesus as one who is meek: "Like a lamb that is led to the slaughter, and like a sheep that before its shearers is silent, so He opened not His mouth" (Isaiah 53:7).

Considerable debate has gone on for years over exactly what part and how much of the cross Jesus carried. Did Jesus carry the entire cross or only the crossbeam (*patibulum*)? Were ropes used to hold His arms in place as He carried the cross? The marks on the Shroud of Turin show two large, somewhat square bruises on the top of each shoulder. This would indicate that a large piece of timber had been laid across the victim's upper back, a manner in which one would carry the *patibulum*. Carrying the entire cross would have been easier if the area where the *patibulum* connects with the *stipes*, or upright piece, was draped over one shoulder. Carrying the entire cross in this way would not have left marks on the top of both shoulders; rather, it would have left marks close to the neck, on the chest, and close to the spine. It is most likely that Jesus carried only the *patibulum*.

Given Jesus' condition from the scourging and the weight of the cross, it is probable that Jesus fell while being led to Golgotha. He would have fallen face first, arms outstretched and holding the crossbeam. The full weight of this beam, approximately one hundred pounds, would have crushed the back of His neck, head, shoulders, and back. This would have forced the crown of thorns deeper into the tissues of His scalp and forehead. It is hard to imagine that any man who had been scourged would have been able to carry a one-hundred-pound piece of lumber, balanced on His shoulders, without securing it in some fashion. Thus falling in this manner would have pulled Jesus' arms against the ropes probably used to secure the beam. Lying face down on the ground, His arms would have been pulled up and backward in a helpless position.

Early Christian writers often compared the sacrifice of Christ to God's call to Abraham to sacrifice Isaac. Here the theologian Romanus Melodus has created a monologue in which God the Father compares the sacrifice of His Son to the sacrifice of Isaac.

In you [Abraham] I foreshadow my plans, For indeed, O just man, you are clearly my figure in relief. Do you wish to know what is to come after you as a result of your deeds? It is for this reason that I had you ascend here, to show you. Just as you did not spare your son because of me, Just so, I shall not spare my son because of all men; But I shall give him to be slain for the sake of the world. . . . In the same way that your Isaac has carried the wood on his shoulders, In the same way, my son will bear the cross on His shoulders. Your great love has revealed to you the future. See now the battering ram attached to the wood; As you see the source of its support, you will understand the mystery. It is by the horns that it holds in the bonds; The horns signify the hands of my son. Set the seal of approval on Him, and I shall guard your son.

It was not long before the Roman centurion in charge of the crucifixion detail realized that Jesus was too weak to carry His own cross. Without help, Jesus surely would have died before His crucifixion. The centurion's charge was to make sure the victim died on the cross, not on the way to the site of crucifixion. So Simon of Cyrene was enlisted to carry the cross to the place of execution, which was called Golgotha (Skull Place).

Domenichino presents the moment at which the Roman centurion commands Simon of Cyrene to carry the cross because Jesus is unable to bear the load. Amid the chaos, the fallen Christ looks at you. And you respond in the words of the hymnist, "Oh, who am I That for my sake My Lord should take Frail flesh and die?"

Christ bore His crossbeam for the sake of the world. In the words of Cyril of Alexandria: They led away the author of life to die—to die for our sake. In a way beyond our understanding, the power of God brought from Christ's passion an end far different from that intended by his enemies. His sufferings served as a snare for death and rendered it powerless. The Lord's death proved to be our restoration to immortality and newness of life. Condemned to death though innocent, he went forward bearing on his shoulders the cross on which he was to suffer. He did this for our sake, taking on himself the punishment that the law justly imposed on sinners. He was cursed for our sake according to the saying of Scripture: "A curse is on everyone who is hanged on a tree." . . . We who have all committed many sins were under that ancient curse for our refusal to obey the law of God. To set us free he who was without sin took that curse on himself. Since he is God who is above all, his sufferings sufficed for all, his death in the flesh was the redemption of all.

Jesus had been beaten and weakened enough that it is probable He fell more than once during His walk, even without the weight of the crossbeam. He had endured extreme emotional anguish, had been kept awake for nearly three days, had been given nothing to eat or drink, had been severely scourged, and was unable to carry His cross or walk a mere one third of a mile, probably without falling several times.

Christ's bearing of the cross is a fundamental image for the Christian life of faith. The Christian dies to believing in himself and everything that is not God and is called to live by faith in the Son of God who loved me and gave Himself for me (Galatians 2:20). Dietrich Bonhoeffer put it this way:

The cross is laid on every Christian. The first Christ-suffering which every man must experience is the call to abandon the attachments of this world. It is the dying of the old man which is the result of his encounter with Christ. As we embark upon discipleship we surrender ourselves to Christ in union with his death—we give over our lives to death. Thus it begins; the cross is not the terrible end to an otherwise god-fearing and happy life, but it meets us at the beginning of our communion with Christ.

When Christ calls a man, he bids him come and die. It may be a death like that of the first disciples who had to leave home and work to follow him, or it may be a death like Luther's, who had to leave the monastery and go out into the world. But it is the same death every time—death in Jesus Christ, the death of the old man at his call.

In Albrecht Dürer's image of Christ bearing the cross, which is part of his *Large Passion*, Jesus is presented as one burdened heavily by the cross and suffering under the torment of His persecutors. Here is the Christ, the Life of the world, beaten down into the dust of the ground by the instrument of His own death. Life is being crushed by sin and death.

Finally, the Gospel reports . . . that as the Lord was being led to his Passion, "they found a certain man of Cyrene named Simon and compelled him to carry the cross." The cross of Christ is the triumph of virtue and a trophy of victory. How blessed is Simon, who deserved to be the first to bear so great a sign of victory! He was compelled to carry the cross before the Lord because the Lord wanted to demonstrate his cross to be a singular grace of that heavenly mystery which is himself: God and man, Logos and flesh, Son of God and Son of man. He was crucified as man but triumphed as God in the mystery of the cross. His suffering was of the flesh, but his glorious victory was divine. Through his cross, Christ defeated both death and the devil. Through the cross, Christ mounted his chariot of victory and chose the four Evangelists, as though horses for his chariot, to announce so great a victory to all the world. Simon of Cyrene therefore was carrying the instrument of this great triumph in his arms. He was a partaker of the Passion of Christ so that he might be a partaker of his resurrection, as the apostle teaches: "If we die with him, we will also live with him. If we endure with him, we will also reign with him." Similarly the Lord himself says in the Gospel: "He who does not take up his cross and follow me cannot be my disciple."

—Chromatius

Francesco di Giorgio Martini's depiction of the crucifixion focuses on the disrobing of Christ. As some of the instruments of His Passion, especially His cross, lie at His feet, the soldiers forcibly remove Jesus' robe, the only thing He could claim as His own, at least from a human perspective. Martini shows Jesus as very much "in the flesh," in every way fully human. Jesus' willingness to suffer this indignity is apparent in His bowed head and meek expression. Little did those at the cross realize that here was paradise restored, but Martini hints at this reality as he places humanity enfleshed in Jesus against the backdrop of the abundant fruit of the Garden of Eden.

Upon arriving at the place of crucifixion, which was called Golgotha, Jesus was stripped of His robes. A full garment had been placed over the gaping wounds of Jesus' back before He was led to Golgotha. This garment would have adhered to the strips of open flesh and the exposed, bleeding muscle on His shoulders, back, arms, chest, buttocks, and legs. The Roman soldiers were not inclined to be gentle. They had a job to do and were professionals. Their intent was to intimidate, which would keep the Jews under control. Here they had a member of a population they did not like, one accused of trying to overthrow Roman rule and authority. As far as they could tell, this Jewish man was not even liked by His own people. They certainly would not have removed the cloth carefully from Jesus' back. Instead, the removal of the cloth would have reopened His wounds.

The believer seeks God where He may be found in mercy. So in the words of Johann Sebastian Bach, the believer hurries to Golgotha.

Hurry, you besieged souls, leave your dens of torment, hurry—where?—to Golgotha! Embrace faith's wings; flee—where?—to the cross's hilltop; your welfare blossoms there!

By the time He arrived at the Place of the Skull, Jesus had suffered unimaginably. He had been mocked, hit, derided, and crowned with thorns. He had been scourged nearly to the point of death. He had traversed the distance from the Praetorium of Pilate to Golgotha, which was outside the city walls. For part of this journey, Jesus had carried the beam of His cross. The suffering of His crucifixion would not be long, but it would be intensely painful. The suffering Son of God and |Son of Man was about to endure His final and most excruciating humiliation.

Consider how it hurts to pull a bandage from a dried wound. Imagine Jesus' agony as the robe is ripped from His body. But He has resolved to trust in His Father and allows His crucifixion to continue. Christ suffered all this agony for you, so that you would be reconciled to God.

For while we were still weak, at the right time Christ died for the ungodly. For one will scarcely die for a righteous person—though perhaps for a good person one would dare even to die—but God shows His love for us in that while we were still sinners, Christ died for us. Since, therefore, we have now been justified by His blood, much more shall we be saved by Him from the wrath of God. For if while we were enemies we were reconciled to God by the death of His Son, much more, now that we are reconciled, shall we be saved by His life. More than that, we also rejoice in God through our Lord Jesus Christ, through whom we have now received reconciliation.

Romans 5:6–11

The man and woman in the foreground of this painting by Giandomenico Tiepolo beckon us to join in contemplating the stripping of Christ. Jesus is clothed in white, emblematic of His divinity. However, His face registers very human pain as the garments are pulled from His body. Christ Jesus, God and man, is stripped as the sacrifice for our sin. So we can sing, "Jesus, Thy blood and righteousness My beauty are, my glorious dress."

As you pray, give thanks for the Suffering Servant, who endures even death on a cross to be God's mercy to you.

It is truly good, right, and salutary that we should at all times and in all places give thanks to You, holy Lord, almighty Father, everlasting God, through Jesus Christ, our Lord, who, out of love for His fallen creation, humbled Himself by taking on the form of a servant, becoming obedient unto death, even death upon a cross. Risen from the dead, He has freed us from eternal death and given us life everlasting. Therefore with angels and archangels and with all the company of heaven we laud and magnify Your glorious name, evermore praising You.

97

The word excruciating *comes from the Latin word* excruciatus, *which means "out of the cross." Out of the cross comes the new covenant promised by God to Israel in Jeremiah 31:31–34:* Behold, the days are coming, declares the LORD, when I will make a new covenant with the house of Israel and the house of Judah, not like the covenant that I made with their fathers on the day when I took them by the hand to bring them out of the land of Egypt, My covenant that they broke, though I was their husband, declares the LORD. But this is the covenant that I will make with the house of Israel after those days, declares the LORD: I will put My law within them, and I will write it on their hearts. And I will be their God, and they shall be My people. And no longer shall each one teach his neighbor and each his brother, saying, "Know the LORD," for they shall all know Me, from the least of them to the greatest, declares the LORD. For I will forgive their iniquity, and I will remember their sin no more. *Through the cross and the forgiveness embedded in it, we know the Lord and He knows us.*

Chapter Four

THe Suffering of Jesus Christ

From the Crucifixion at Golgotha to the Burial

Your cords of love, my Savior,
Bind me to You forever,
I am no longer mine.
To You I gladly tender
All that my life can render
And all I have to You resign.

The History of Crucifixion

The Gospels do not show great interest in the details of crucifixion itself as they proclaim Jesus' Passion. To understand the reluctance of the evangelists to expound on the cruelty of crucifixion, one must recognize that they were very familiar with this form of capital punishment and it repulsed them. Crucifixion would have been witnessed all too frequently as a religious-political punishment that was practiced by the Romans to excess.

The use of crucifixion predates the time of Christ by hundreds of years. Historians refer to crucifixion as far back as the time of the Assyrians, the Scythians, and the Taurians. The historians Herodotus and Ctesias attributed the origins of this vile

As you pray this prayer, rejoice that reflection on the Passion of Christ leads you to receive the benefits of His crucifixion as they come to you in His body broken for you and His blood poured out on your lips. O Lord, in this wondrous Sacrament [of the Lord's Supper] You have left us a remembrance of Your passion. Grant that we may so receive the sacred mystery of Your body and blood that the fruits of Your redemption may continually be manifest in us; for You live and reign with the Father and the Holy Spirit, one God, now and forever. Amen.

Peter Paul Rubens invites us to ponder the suffering of Jesus, which He undertook for us. The dark and insidious background echoes Isaiah 49:21, which prophesies that the Christ would be "left all alone." Jesus bore the rejection of sinful men by Himself; His Father could not stand with Him.

While the Romans may have perfected crucifixion, God undid the power of death by transforming the cross into the tree of life.

Christ wishes us to be grafted into his death like a shoot of a tree, so that our roots may draw sustenance from his, producing holy branches and living fruit. And if we consult the scriptures about the stock into which we have to be grafted and the kind of tree it is, we find this text concerning wisdom: "She is a tree of life to those who hope in her and put their trust in her, as in the Lord" [Proverbs 3:18]. This tree of life into which we have to be grafted is Christ "who is the power and the wisdom of God" [1 Corinthians 1:24]—Christ who by his death, that unprecedented gift of divine love, became for us a tree of life.

—Origen

punishment to the Persians. Herodotus gives a vivid account of the Athenian General Xanthippus crucifying Artayctes for religious offenses by nailing him to planks and leaving him to hang. Then Xanthippus proceeded to stone Artayctes' son before his eyes. In the third century before Christ, Plautos mentions crucifixion as a punishment for the lower classes. Its use was rampant among the Numidians and especially the Carthaginians. The popularity and use of crucifixion spread during the conquests of Alexander the Great, and he is credited with bringing the practice to the Romans. It is said that though the Romans did not invent crucifixion, they perfected it.

Crucifixion was an extremely effective means of waging war and securing peace. It was used to wear down cities under siege by breaking the will of surrounded soldiers and townspeople. It was used, often excessively, to secure peace and control provinces under Roman military control, especially rebellious provinces such as the Jewish lands. Often whole cities or groups of soldiers or rebels would surrender after witnessing the crucifixion of friends and comrades. For example, threats to crucify one Jewish prisoner during the siege of Jerusalem caused the entire garrison of Machaerus to surrender. Crucifixion also was used effectively as a threat to prevent mutiny among Roman troops. The Jewish historian Josephus, who was an advisor to the Roman emperor Titus, described crucifixion as "the most wretched of deaths."

Evidence points to the fact that crucifixion was used by societies prior to the Romans. However, the Romans perfected this punishment as a means to dominate conquered peoples. Crosses were instruments of torture; however, through the death of Christ, the cross is transformed into the vehicle for life and salvation. Even the earliest depictions of the cross, such as this ivory relief from the fifth century, illustrate this transformation. Here Christ is depicted open-eyed and alive. Ultimately, the cross could not conquer the Son of God.

O crucified Jesus, Son of the Father, conceived by the Holy Spirit, born of the Virgin Mary, eternal Word of God, we worship you. O crucified Jesus, holy temple of God, dwelling place of the Most High, gate of heaven, burning flame of love, we worship you. O crucified Jesus, sanctuary of justice and love, full of kindness, source of all faithfulness, we worship you. O crucified Jesus, ruler of every heart, in you are the treasures of wisdom and knowledge, in you dwells all the fullness of the Godhead, we worship you. Jesus, lamb of God, have mercy on us. Jesus, bearer of our sins, have mercy on us. Jesus, redeemer of the world, grant us peace.

Antonello da Messina has suspended the criminals crucified with Christ from trees. In contrast to their tortured positions on impossibly curved trees, Christ appears serene in death, nailed to a perfectly straight cross.

Ancient writers mention only briefly the act of crucifixion. The scarcity of information about crucifixion in the ancient world proves that the learned scribes of the earliest societies had a deep aversion to this cruel, terrifying, and vile punishment. Once witnessed, the mere mention of the cross evoked sufficient mental images to preclude the need for any written description of the process. Indeed, some of the most graphic details of crucifixion are found in the Gospels of Matthew, Mark, Luke, and John.

Pre-Roman crucifixions dating to the Persians are described as running a long post or tree between the victim's legs, thus impaling and disemboweling the victim. Death was violent and came quickly. As the process of crucifixion evolved, executioners discovered that suspending victims on a tree or planks of wood allowed them to hang for longer periods, thus prolonging the demonstration and agony of death.

O Cross, more worthy than cedar, on you the life of the world was nailed, on you Christ has triumphed: death has destroyed death! Glory to you, Jesus, Savior, your cross gives us life! Behold the tree of life where the new Adam offers his blood to gather all people into one Body: Come, let us adore! Behold the tree of life where the Savior of the world holds out his hands to embrace us all, in his forgiveness: Come, let us adore! Behold the tree of life where the Father's beloved opens the gates of the kingdom: Come, let us adore! Behold the tree of life where love cries that it is forsaken to give hope to all the unloved: Come, let us adore! Behold the tree of life where the Son of Man gives the Spirit while breathing his last within the Father's hands: Come, let us adore! Behold the tree of life where the light of the world shines in the darkness in order to accomplish the Passover of the universe: Come, let us adore! . . . Behold the tree of life where the innocent man bears our sins in order to reconcile earth and heaven: Come, let us adore!

Set your hopes only upon the cross. Call to mind the humbling things that were then taking place. Then you will cast out as dust all rage by the recollection of the things that were done to him.

Consider his words. Consider his actions. Remember that he is Lord and you are his servant. Remember that he is suffering for you, and for you individually. You may be suffering only on your own behalf. He is suffering on behalf of all by whom he had been crucified. You may be suffering in the presence of a few. He suffers in the sight of the whole city and of the whole people of the covenant, both of strangers and those of the holy land, to all of whom he spoke merciful words.

Even his disciples forsook him. This was most distressing to him. Those who previously paid him mind suddenly deserted him. Meanwhile his enemies and foes, having captured him and put him on a cross, insulted him, reviled him, mocked him, derided him and scoffed at him. See the Jews and soldiers rejecting him from below. See how he was set between two thieves on either side, and even the thieves insulted him and upbraided him.

—*John Chrysostom*

Roman-era crosses consisted of two pieces of rough unfinished wood. Because lumber most likely was of great value in the Near East, it can be assumed that each piece was used for numerous crucifixions. The two pieces of wood consisted of the upright post (*stipes*) and the horizontal crossbeam (*patibulum*). These were not finished pieces of wood and may have resembled railroad ties. The *stipes* of the "latin cross" extended well beyond the victim's head, while that of the "tau cross" extended only a short distance beyond the crossbeam. It is believed that the tau cross was the type used in Palestine during the period when Christ's crucifixion occurred.

A banner (*titulus*), carried by one of the Roman guards from the crucifixion detail, announced the offenses or crimes of the condemned man. The *titulus* was affixed to the extension of the *stipes* beyond the *patibulum* at the time of crucifixion. In Jesus' case, this *titulus* announced Jesus' offenses in Hebrew, Latin, and Greek—at that time the three primary languages of the land.

The *stipes* most likely remained at the place of crucifixion permanently. It had to be secured sufficiently so it remained upright while a man was hung on it, writhing in pain, struggling to free himself. It is believed that the *patibulum*, which weighed approximately one hundred pounds, was the only part of the cross to be transported by the condemned victim to the place of death. After being scourged or beaten, the *patibulum* would be placed across the top of the victim's shoulders. His arms and hands, outstretched in a manner similar to being crucified, were tied to the crossbeam with ropes. Then the centurion and the Roman crucifixion detail would lead the victim through the streets for all to see. If the victim fell during this procession, he could not protect himself with his hands, so he would fall to the ground face first, the weight of the crossbeam pushing down on his head, neck, and upper back.

Andrea Mantegna provides a historically accurate depiction of Golgotha as a regular place for crucifixions. The holes in the pavement denote permanent places to erect crosses. It is a prominent place on the way out of Jerusalem. All who pass see the vail of death among the women weighted against humanity's indifference as the young soldiers cast dice for Jesus' tunic.

This depiction of the crucifixion provides a very Roman-looking cast as witnesses of Christ's death, especially in the depiction of the centurion. Once again, Christ is depicted not in great suffering but as alive and victorious over His enemies.

Romans put crucifixion first (worst) in their list of approved forms of the death penalty. Other acceptable and frequently practiced forms of capital punishment included burning, decapitation, and exposure to wild beasts. The Romans, though disgusted with the horrifying cruelty of crucifixion, took it for granted that criminals had to be executed in this manner. Crucifixion was widespread and frequent in the ancient world, but the cultured literary world wanted little or nothing to do with it and as a general rule kept quiet about it. The mention of crucifixion without the explicit details sufficed in most writings.

Jesus, I will ponder now
On Your holy passion;
With Your Spirit me endow
For such meditation.
Grant that I in love and faith
May the image cherish
Of Your suff'ring, pain, and death
That I may not perish.

Make me see Your great distress,
Anguish, and affliction,
Bonds and stripes and wretchedness
And Your crucifixion;
Make me see how scourge and rod,
Spear and nails did wound You,
How for them You died, O God,
Who with thorns had crowned You.

Yet, O Lord, not thus alone
Make me see Your passion,
But its cause to me make known
And its termination.
Ah! I also and my sin
Wrought Your deep affliction;
This indeed the cause has been
Of Your crucifixion.

Grant that I Your passion view
With repentant grieving.
Let me not bring shame to You
By unholy living.
How could I refuse to shun
Ev'ry sinful pleasure
Since for me God's only Son
Suffered without measure?

If my sins give me alarm
And my conscience grieve me,
Let Your cross my fear disarm;
Peace of conscience give me.
Help me see forgiveness won
By Your holy passion.
If for me He slays His Son,
God must have compassion!

Graciously my faith renew;
Help me bear my crosses,
Learning humbleness from You,
Peace mid pain and losses.
May I give You love for love!
Hear me, O my Savior,
That I may in heav'n above
Sing Your praise forever.

Death came slowly and with a great deal of pain and suffering. Roman executioners became experts in the process of scourging and honed the art of causing the most pain over the longest period of time. The norm for crucifixion, and most other capital punishments, included scourging (flogging or beating) beforehand. Then the victim was forced to carry the crossbeam, and sometimes the entire cross, to his place of execution.

The form of execution varied considerably, depending on the whim of the executioner. According to Lucius Seneca (55 BC–AD 37), a Spanish-born Roman historian and rhetorician, crosses and victims could be positioned in many different ways: some victims were crucified with their heads toward the ground, while some were suspended with their heads up and arms outstretched. Often victims were tortured immediately before crucifixion and subjected to sadistic practices while hanging on the cross. Sometimes bodies were burned at sundown as human torches for all to see. At other times, bodies were left hanging for days. After death, the remains were thrown into open pits without burial.

Josephus provides a glimpse into the varied ways of Roman crucifixion. He was an eyewitness to the punishment of Jewish fugitives who attempted to escape from Jerusalem when it was besieged by the Romans in AD 71. He wrote that Emperor Titus, though he felt pity for the fugitives, allowed his soldiers to have their way with the captives. They were nailed in different positions to the crosses by way of jest. The number of victims was so great that there was not enough room for the crosses and not enough crosses for the bodies. Similarly, during the revolt of Spartacus against the Romans in 71 BC, more than six thousand crosses with crucified victims lined the road from Capua to Rome (approximately one hundred miles).

The movement and gestures of Mary and John (or possibly Joseph of Arimathea) as he carries Jesus' body in this thirteenth-century sculpture communicate deep emotion. John stoops under the weight of Jesus' limp body, even as Mary tenderly holds Jesus' hand, perhaps ready to place it against her cheek.

But it is by dying that your shepherd proved his love for you. When danger threatens his sheep and he sees himself unable to protect them, he chooses to die rather than to see calamity overtake his flock. What am I saying? Could Life himself die unless he chose to? Could anyone take life from its author against his will? He himself declared, "I have power to lay down my life, and I have power to take it up again; no one takes it from me" [John 10:18]. To die, therefore, was his own choice. Immortal though he was, he allowed himself to be put to death.

By allowing himself to be taken captive, he overpowered his opponent. By submitting, he overcame him. By his own execution, he penalized his enemy, and by dying he opened the door to the conquest of death for his whole flock. And so the good Shepherd lost none of his sheep when he laid down his life for them. He did not desert them but kept them safe. He did not abandon them but called them to follow him, leading them by the way of death through the lowlands of this passing world to the pastures of life.

—*Peter Chrysologus*

The figures of John and the two Marys in this painting by Eustache Le Sueur exhibit anxious yearning as those closest to the Savior watch Him suffer. Jesus looks to heaven, while His mother, His beloved disciple John, and Mary Magdalene "fix [their] eyes on Jesus, the author and perfecter of our faith, who for the joy set before Him endured the cross, scorning its shame" (Hebrews 12:2 NIV).

As a means of capital punishment, crucifixion was outlawed in the Roman Empire in AD 341 by Emperor Constantine. Since then the practice of crucifixion has been seen from time to time. On February 5, 1597, Father Paul Miki, a Jesuit missionary, and twenty-three of his companions were crucified together in Nagasaki, Japan. There are accounts of prisoners held by the Austro-Hungarian army who were crucified while being held captive (mid-1800s). World War II prisoners at the Dachau concentration camp (1930s) were tortured and killed by crucifixion while those who held them documented the events in the name of scientific experimentation. The cross in early Christianity was not the symbol of salvation that it has become today. Instead, it was a highly offensive symbol that imposed a tremendous burden on the earliest preachers of Christ and the faith. Crucifixion was a form of capital punishment generally reserved for slaves, traitors, deserters, and revolutionaries, among whom Jesus was numbered. His death by crucifixion implied that Christ was a criminal, not a king; a revolutionary, not the Savior; a slave, not a ruler. As Paul states, the cross was a scandal and an offense. As far as the archaeological evidence indicates, imagery of Jesus crucified or of the cross was not helpful or appealing in the Early Church's mission of proclaiming Christ as the Savior of the world. It was not until the fifth and sixth centuries that the crucifix became a symbol of the Christian faith. The earliest crucifixes depicted Jesus not as a suffering and reviled man, but standing in front of the cross with arms stretched toward heaven. He was pictured in His glory. Not until several centuries later is Jesus depicted in the fullness of His Passion and death—as a man who was crucified on a cross.

Often crucifixes or artistic presentations of Jesus on the cross portray a clean white body, arms outstretched, hands and feet affixed with nails, the body displayed in a visually inoffensive pose. In reality, Jesus' body would have been torn from the scourging, covered with blood, and twisted into a visually offensive posture by its attachment to the cross.

Why is Jesus on the cross pictured in an almost sterile manner? Perhaps it is because we do not want to face the reality that humanity rejected the Son of God and perpetrated such a cruel death. But the cross only tells part of the story. Our salvation does not rest in the crucifixion alone, but in Jesus' death and resurrection. In fact, our Savior's entire ministry is centered in His death and resurrection. The crucifixion is one key part of our salvation, but not the sole or final part.

While crucifixes and depictions of the crucified Jesus should portray the harsh reality of the cross as the instrument on which the God-man died, they should ultimately point to His resurrection. In Baptism we are buried with Christ into His death and resurrection, and because of this we will participate in the resurrection of the dead on the Last Day.

Now before the Feast of the Passover, when Jesus knew that His hour had come to depart out of this world to the Father, having loved His own who were in the world, He loved them to the end. During supper, when the devil had already put it into the heart of Judas Iscariot, Simon's son, to betray Him, Jesus, knowing that the Father had given all things into His hands, and that He had come from God and was going back to God, rose from supper. He laid aside His outer garments, and taking a towel, tied it around His waist. Then He poured water into a basin and began to wash the disciples' feet and to wipe them with the towel that was wrapped around Him. He came to Simon Peter, who said to Him, "Lord, do You wash my feet?" Jesus answered him, "What I am doing you do not understand now, but afterward you will understand." . . .

Jesus said, "Now is the Son of Man glorified, and God is glorified in Him. If God is glorified in Him, God will also glorify Him in Himself, and glorify Him at once. Little children, yet a little while I am with you. You will seek Me, and just as I said to the Jews, so now I also say to you, 'Where I am going you cannot come.' A new commandment I give to you, that you love one another: just as I have loved you, you also are to love one another. By this all people will know that you are My disciples, if you have love for one another.

John 13:1–7, 31–35

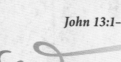

The Process of Crucifixion

What actually happens to a person's body in the process of dying on a cross? How did Jesus suffer? How cruel was the experience of crucifixion?

At Golgotha (Skull Place), the site of execution, Jesus was offered a mixture of wine and myrrh called gall. This bitter mixture traditionally was offered as a mild analgesic to dull the senses before the act of crucifixion. Today, gall would be equivalent to a weak mixture of acetaminophen in a wine solution. Once this mixture touched His lips, Jesus refused to drink it. More ceremonial than effective, gall would have done little to relieve the pain that followed.

Upon arriving at Golgotha, Jesus was thrown on top of the *patibulum*, which would have been placed on the ground after being carried to the site by Simon. This action would have forced dirt into the wounds on Jesus' back, head, and legs, causing the blood to coagulate, harden, and dry. The crown of thorns would have been forced deeper into His scalp, creating more intense pain and further bleeding.

The cross height, as well as its design, have been debated for centuries. As indicated earlier, the tau cross (*crux humulis*), or low cross, which resembles a capital *T*, was used most commonly in that region of the Roman Empire. A latin cross (*crux sublimis*), which was taller and shaped like a lowercase *t*, would have required special preparation. Because the crucifixion of Jesus was not planned and followed trials and a verdict rendered in just a few short hours, the fixed upright *stipes* of Golgotha would most likely have been employed in this hasty situation.

The cross used for Jesus' death was the cross of criminals. But His cross was destined by God to be the instrument of His mercy, as shown by the following stanzas from the traditional Good Friday hymn "The Royal Banners Forward Go."

On whose hard arms, so widely flung,
The weight of this world's ransom hung,
The price of humankind to pay
And spoil the spoiler of his prey.

O tree of beauty, tree most fair,
Ordained those holy limbs to bear:
Gone is thy shame, each crimsoned bough
Proclaims the King of Glory now.

Christ, strong in appearance, hangs on a crude instrument of torture and death, literally the *tree* of the cross. The circlets above the crossbeam reveal the soldiers arguing over Christ's garments, exposing the chaos that ensues from human attempts to silence God and His ways of mercy. Amid this chaos, the hand of the Father points to His Son, the Lamb who takes away the sin of the world (John 1:29). Mary Magdalene clings to the cross, the tree of life that brings healing to the nations. Unlike other scenes of the crucifixion, John and Jesus' mother are not distraught. Instead, Mary clothes her naked Son, garments in which humanity will be clothed. And John writes his Gospel of peace and victory through the cross, "so that you may believe that Jesus is the Christ, the Son of God, and that by believing you may have life in His name" (John 20:31).

Rich in symbolism, this painting depicts the cross as the tree of life, ripe with the fruit of God's fulfillment of His promises. Growing from the branches of the tree of the cross and surrounding its base are (counterclockwise from lower right): a hammer smashing a skull, which symbolizes Jesus' victory over death; a blindfolded man and an altar, which symbolizes the unbelieving Jews and the fulfillment in Christ of the redemption promised through Moses and the sacrificial system; a skull, snake, and apple, which represent the defeat of the devil, temptation, and sin; the sword of punishment, which Christ accepted in our place; the figures of Adam and Eve recall that Jesus' death brings redemption for the sin in the garden; the hand with a key represents the authority to open the kingdom of heaven; the hand of blessing; the Church, the mystical lamb, the New Testament, the chalice, and the woman all evoke the promises of God fulfilled through Christ in the Church and in Word and Sacraments.

The *stipes* has been estimated to be approximately six or seven feet in height. At this height, the *patibulum* could be affixed quite easily to the *stipes*, and the feet would have been approximately one foot off the ground. Thus the feet of the victim could have been easily attached to the *stipes* with only a slight bend of the legs—an easy task for the Roman detail. The victim's mouth would have hung at a level even with or slightly lower than the level of the *patibulum*, approximately seven feet off the ground.

When Jesus said, "I thirst," He was offered a drink on a sponge. Most likely this drink was *posca*, a sour wine mixed with water (and perhaps egg), a drink common to Roman soldiers. The Roman soldier's short javelin was approximately three feet long, with a metal spear tip adding another foot to the overall length. When held at arm's length, the javelin with the sponge attached would have reached approximately seven feet into the air from the ground.

While the Roman guards carried out the task of positioning the cross, Jesus Himself really set up His cross. Consider the words of the great hymnwriter Ephrem the Syrian:

He who was also the carpenter's glorious son set up his cross above death's all-consuming maw, and led the human race into the dwelling place of life. Since a tree had brought about the downfall of our race, it was upon a tree that we crossed over to the realm of life. Bitter was the branch that had once been grafted upon that ancient tree, but sweet the young shoot that has now been grafted in, the shoot in which we are meant to recognize the Lord whom no creation can resist.

We give glory to you, Lord, who raised up your cross to span the jaws of death like a bridge by which souls might pass from the region of the dead to the land of the living.

In his comments on John 8:28 ("So Jesus said to them, 'When you have lifted up the Son of Man, then you will know that I am He, and that I do nothing on My own authority, but speak just as the Father taught Me.'"), Martin Luther states that Christ's crucifixion is the revelation of God through the suffering Son of Man.

And now He says: "You will not know Me until I have been lifted up, until I have died and perished." As though He were to say that through His death He would conquer all, namely, the devil, sin, and death; that He would present and give to us all righteousness, wisdom, power, and every good; that He would become Lord over all and tread every evil on earth underfoot; and that the Holy Spirit would not be given until He, in His body, had overcome all and had gained the victory. On the cross He was opposed by the highest power, the greatest wisdom, holiness, riches, and might, yes, by all that was rated high in the world. Furthermore, our own sin, the Law, death, the devil, and Moses with his whole nation rise up against this Man; every good and every evil—such as sin, death, the devil, and hell—set themselves up against Him. And these must first be drowned in His blood, captured and vanquished. Death assailed Him; sin also pressed Him hard, as though He were the vilest malefactor on earth. But death could not devour Him, for He rose from the dead. Sin also laid hold of Him, but it could not overcome Him. All the great lords and prelates arrayed themselves against Him, but they could not gain the victory over Him; on the third day He rose from the dead.

For many years exegetes and scientists alike have argued about the method and placement of the nails or spikes used to affix Christ's arms and legs to the cross. Many exegetes believe Jesus' arms were suspended with nails driven through His hands. In 1953, P. Barbet conducted an experiment in which he tied weights on cadaver arms to determine if using a nail through the web spaces of the hand, between the wrist bones, or elsewhere could hold the weight of a crucified man. He determined that the division of weight between two oblique and symmetrical forces means that each point is bearing considerably more than half of the total weight. Thus nails placed into the hands would need to hold firmly in place and support the equivalent of nearly 240 pounds per nail. He concluded that a nail driven through only the soft tissues of the hand would not hold the weight of a man suspended and writhing on a cross. The nail would have been pulled through the full thickness of the hand if it was driven only through these tissues. However, Barbet did conclude that the area between the bones of the wrist and the end of the forearm's radial bone is sufficiently strong to hold the weight of a man during crucifixion. In their studies of anatomy, the Romans considered the wrist to be part of the hand. Thus as the Gospels indicate, the nails would have been driven through the wrists (considered as part of the hand), which is also the location of the nail wounds in the hands of the figure on the Shroud of Turin.

Giovanni Canavesio expresses visually the reality of the nailing of Christ's hands and feet to the cross. Nearly the entire Roman contingent participates, and Canavesio captures the physical effort required of the soldiers. In contrast, Jesus appears completely passive. While the picture is alive with the struggle and exertion of the men crucifying Jesus, the area surrounding the cross is a barren wilderness, a rocky outgrowth devoid of life. Jesus' ministry ends where it began—in the desert wilderness, tempted by Satan, and with the wild animals. Why does our Savior not resist? Because "man shall not live by bread alone, but by every word that comes from the mouth of God" (Matthew 4:4).

According to Martin Luther, the life of the world hangs in the balance because of the One who hangs on the cross: death for life, life for death.

He is punished; we have peace. I, you, all of us have angered God; for that he needed to atone, so that we might be redeemed from sin and obtain peace. He suffers; we go free. The indulgence hawkers assured us that your desperate beads of sweat and gross carousings would, by the pope's indulgences, be freed from pain and punishment. They directed us to believe that our souls must suffer in purgatory, when in reality (even as they spoke) they already had departed in grace and love. Does not the prophet say, "The chastisement of our peace was upon him," in order that it might be well with us and we might enjoy good days? This great love and grace no person should ever so shamefully forget. The great harm the devil caused us in paradise has been healed by Christ's wounds.

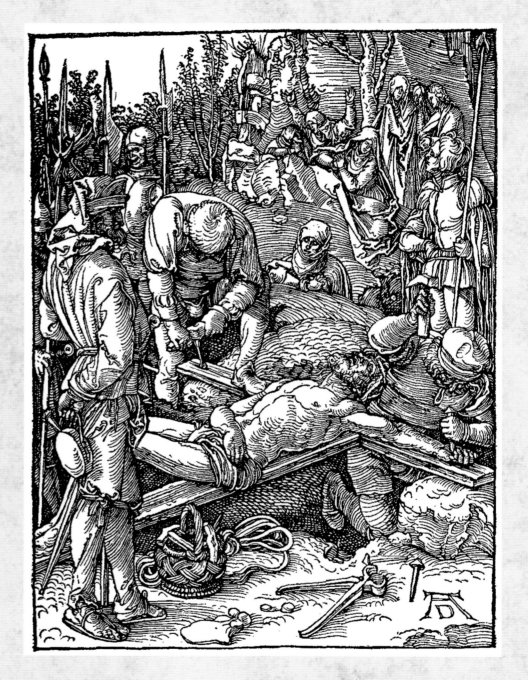

Albrecht Dürer captures the methodical nature of the soldiers' work as they nail Christ to the cross. Much like a craftsman fashioning metalwork or pottery, the soldiers dutifully fulfill their calling and unwittingly craft the instrument of the world's redemption.

The spike or nail used to affix the victim to the cross would have been five to seven inches in length with a square shaft about three-eighths of an inch in diameter. It would have been slightly thinner, but longer, than a modern railroad spike. Most likely the edges of the shaft would have been squared off.

The placement of these spikes was intended to pass through, or crush, the nerves without disrupting the blood vessels. At the top of the palm there is a crease formed when bringing the thumb and the little finger together. This crease is at the junction of the short muscles of the thumb and the little finger. Behind this ridge and approximately one-inch wide is a thick, fibrous ligament connected to the bones on the little finger side and to the bones on the thumb side. This transverse carpal ligament forms a tunnel at the wrist to protect the median nerve that connects to the thumb, fingers, and hand. The median nerve is the primary sensory and motor nerve of the hand and most of the fingers. The release of this ligament today is commonly referred to as carpal tunnel release. Bringing the thumb and little finger together creates a hollow, or soft spot, just above the carpal ligament at the main folding line of the wrist. This hollow area, referred to as Destot's space, allows easy access for placing a nail through the wrist bones. Passing a nail through this space would not break any bones and would provide full weight-bearing ability to the carpal ligament. The nail would have crushed, or partially severed, the median nerve, causing intense and continuous pain. Crushing the median nerve would have caused the thumb to flex in toward the palm of the hand and created a clawlike contraction of the index, long, and ring fingers. With the squared-off spikes holding the arms in place, the continuous pain from the crushed median nerve would have intensified with any movement of the arms or body.

The image on the Shroud of Turin reveals thumbs retracted into the palms with only four fingers on each hand visible. A nail driven into Destot's space would cause severe pain but would damage only venous structures with very slow blood loss. This is because the arteries of the hand run on both sides of the wrist. After entering the hand, they arch further down in the palm rather than across Destot's space. No damage to arterial blood flow would have occurred from spikes driven into the body in this area. Thus rapid blood loss was avoided, serving to prolong the agony of crucifixion. The Romans were experts at crucifixion and knew how to cause the most pain with the least amount of blood loss, making this the most painful and drawn-out process of humiliation, suffering, and death imaginable.

The possibility of using ropes to hold the arms of the victim to the *patibulum* has been voiced through the years. If the nails or spikes were placed correctly, there would be no need for ropes tied around the *patibulum* to support the arms. If the nails were placed in an area that would not hold the weight of a crucified man, then ropes would be necessary to keep the victim affixed to the cross. There is no mention in the Scriptures of ropes being used, so it is assumed that Jesus did not have ropes to support Him.

Jesus' arms would have been affixed to the cross with a little bend at His elbows because this, too, helped prolong the suffering. As was proven in horrific studies in concentration camps during the Second World War, the Romans knew that if the arms were affixed straight or directly above the victim, he would die more quickly. Since the inability to breathe correctly is the main cause of death during crucifixion, the slight bend in the elbows allowed the victim to adjust his chest configuration and continue to breathe, thus prolonging the suffering.

Once Christ's arms were affixed to the *patibulum*, the Roman detail would have picked up the ends of the *patibulum* to affix the crossbeam to the *stipes*. Christ would have been suspended by His wrists while they lifted the crossbeam up and over the top of the *stipes* and dropped it, and Him, into place. The total weight of the *patibulum* and Jesus would not have been more than three hundred and twenty-five pounds. Lifting the crucified victim, as well as the *patibulum*, easily would have been accomplished by an experienced crucifixion detail, especially if the *stipes* was not more than six or seven feet high. The shear agony of this procedure is hard to fathom.

When our Lord was handed over to the will of his cruel foes, they ordered him, in mockery of his royal dignity, to carry the instrument of his own torture. This was done to fulfill the prophecy of Isaiah: "A child is born for us, a son is given to us; sovereignty is laid on his shoulders." To the wicked, the sight of the Lord carrying his own cross was indeed an object of derision. But to the faithful a great mystery was revealed, for the cross was destined to become the scepter of his power. Here was the majestic spectacle of a glorious conqueror mightily overthrowing the hostile forces of the devil and nobly bearing the trophy of his victory. On the shoulders of his invincible patience he carried the sign of salvation for all the kingdoms of the earth to worship, as if on that day he would strengthen all his future disciples by the symbol of his work and say to them, "Anyone who does not take up his cross and follow me is not worthy of me" [Matthew 10:38].

—Leo the Great

A group of men hoist the crucified Christ from the ground, where He had been nailed to the cross. Mary Magdalene and Jesus' mother faint as they witness the act. Peter Paul Rubens uses strong diagonals both in the cross and the figures to communicate the distress and chaos of the moment. Darkness encompasses the chaos, but light emanates from the serene Christ, His dangling feet supported by one soldier as others struggle to lift the cross into place. Those who do evil hate the light and will not enter it for fear that their deeds will be exposed (see John 3:20). But here at the cross, the prophetic truth of Jesus' words rings out loud and clear, "I am the light of the world. Whoever follows Me will never walk in darkness, but will have the light of life" (John 8:12).

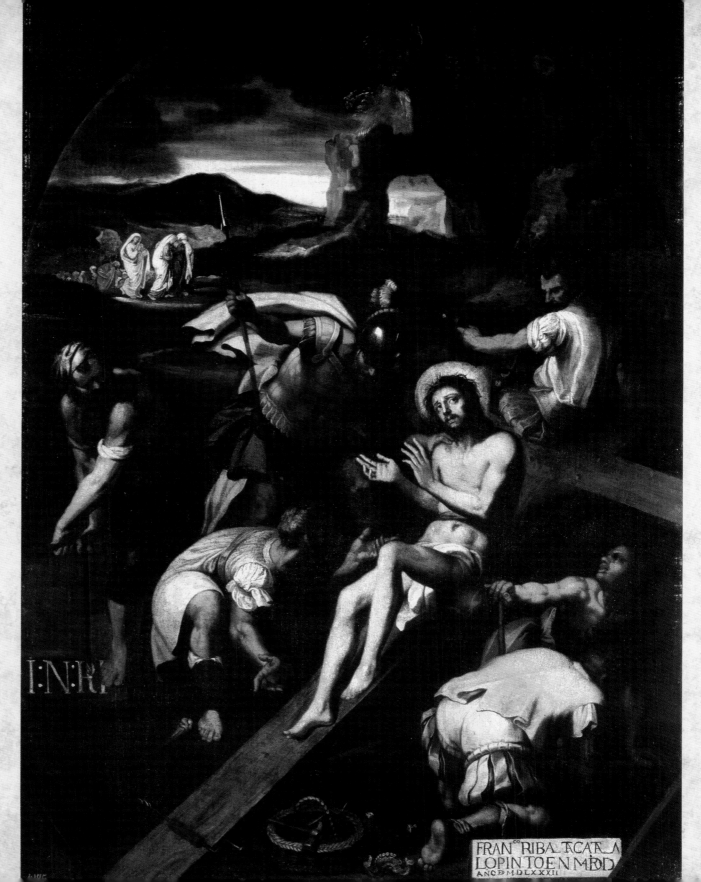

Francisco Ribalta shows Jesus willingly positioning Himself upon the cross. Looking toward heaven and away from the scene in which He is at the center, Christ's peaceful pose and expression contrasts with the soldiers' deliberate work, including the preparation of the inscription INRI, "Jesus of Nazareth, King of the Jews." The evil of this enterprise is hidden in the ordinary responsibilities of human beings, which causes us to ask, in the words of Isaac Watts: "Was it for crimes that I had done He groaned upon the tree? Amazing pity, grace unknown, and love beyond degree!"

The Romans also knew that the agony of death could be prolonged if the feet were nailed to the cross. If the feet were left to dangle, the victim experienced a hasty death. To prolong the process, the feet were nailed or tied to the *stipes*. The nails placed through the feet had to support the weight of a man while he pushed up to breathe.

Where the feet of the victim were placed on the cross—one on top of the other, side by side, or on each side of the cross—has been a matter of discussion. Barbet and others have postulated that each foot was affixed to its side of the cross. Other scholars feel the feet were nailed one over the other or even separately to the front of the cross. Some have postulated the use of one nail in each foot, regardless of their positioning. The Shroud of Turin reveals a victim with the left foot over the top of the right, implying the use of only one nail.

The nail used to affix the feet would have been the same length as those in the wrists and would have been placed as strategically as they were. Because a key artery moves behind the first long bone of the foot at the top of the arch, the nail would have passed between the second and third long bones. Thus only venous blood, not arterial blood, would have been disrupted.

A nail placed in this area of the body would have passed through or come in contact with the deep nerve (peroneal) of the foot, as well as branches of both the medial and lateral nerves (plantar). A nail placed in Lisfranc's space, which separates the upper foot and ankle bones (tarsals) from the long bones (metatarsals) of the foot, would hold the weight of a man while pushing himself up, but it would not break any bones. The legs would have been slightly bent at the knees to secure the feet to the cross. As with the arms, damage to the nerves of the feet would have created lightning-bolt flashes of pain along the entire length of Jesus' legs. His body weight and any movement around the square nails would intensify the pain.

The Romans used the act of crucifixion as a show of force and a deterrent to crime and rebellion. The victim's body would hang on the cross from hours to days, even after death had occurred. The victims were suspended off the ground on a high point in the city or along a busy road so citizens and those passing by would witness this demonstration of force and intimidation.

After Jesus' era, the Romans developed additional tools to lengthen the suffering of crucifixion. The use of a small piece of wood, called a suppedaneum, under the feet became common. This enabled the victim to push up on his legs to breathe, thus prolonging the process of dying. Another simple device used to prolong death was a small piece of wood provided as a seat for the victim. Called a sedile or sedulum, it, too, provided the victim with respite from the difficulty of breathing. Neither device prevented death but served only to prolong the process.

This hymn text by Stephen Starke captures Dietrich Bonhoeffer's assertion that the tree of life in the Garden of Eden is God, who as the source of life is always at the center of the existence of all things. When our sin detached us from the tree of life, God provided another as the source of life.

The tree of life with ev'ry good
In Eden's holy orchard stood,
And of its fruit so pure and sweet
God let the man and woman eat.
Yet in this garden also grew
Another tree, of which they knew;
Its lovely limbs with fruit adorned
Against whose eating God had warned.

The stillness of that sacred grove
Was broken, as the serpent strove
With tempting voice Eve to beguile
And Adam too by sin defile.
O day of sadness when the breath
Of fear and darkness, doubt and death,
Its awful poison first displayed
Within the world so newly made.

What mercy God showed to our race,
A plan of rescue by His grace:
In sending One from woman's seed,
The One to fill our greatest need—
For on a tree uplifted high
His only Son for sin would die,
Would drink the cup of scorn and dread
To crush the ancient serpent's head!

Now from that tree of Jesus' shame
Flows life eternal in His name;
For all who trust and will believe,
Salvation's living fruit receive.
And of this fruit so pure and sweet
The Lord invites the world to eat,
To find within this cross of wood
The tree of life with ev'ry good.

Raising Jesus' cross to its upright position was one of the most searing experiences in the Passion. As He was lifted up, gravity would have pulled Jesus' body down on the nails in His hands and feet. The whiteness of Jesus' body in this painting by Jörg Breu evokes the searing pain.

This fresco by Tommaso Massacio offers a two-dimensional perspective on the crucifixion. Christ is placed within the arms of God the Father, who is holding His Son's cross. Through His sacrifice, Christ drinks the cup of suffering from His Father and accomplishes His Father's will. Mary and the apostle John witness the crucifixion. The two figures kneeling at either pillar outside the archway depict the two donors of the fresco. The sarcophagus and skeleton below the figures are actually part of the painting. As a whole, the fresco encompasses the earthly and heavenly realms, and it positions Christ and His sacrifice on the cross as that which joins the mortal body with God the Father.

Behold, My servant shall act wisely;
   He shall be high and lifted up,
   and shall be exalted.

As many were astonished at you—
   His appearance was so marred,
   beyond human semblance,
   and His form beyond that
   of the children of mankind—
so shall He sprinkle many nations;
   kings shall shut their mouths
   because of Him;
for that which has not been told
them they see,
   and that which they have not
   heard they understand.

Who has believed what they
heard from us?
   And to whom has the arm of
   the LORD been revealed?

For He grew up before Him
like a young plant,
   and like a root out of dry ground;
He had no form or majesty
that we should look at Him,
   and no beauty that we
   should desire Him.

He was despised and rejected by men;
   a man of sorrows, and
   acquainted with grief;
and as one from whom men
hide their faces
   He was despised,

and we esteemed Him not.
Surely He has borne our griefs
   and carried our sorrows;
yet we esteemed Him stricken,
   smitten by God, and afflicted.

But He was wounded for
our transgressions;
   He was crushed for our iniquities;
upon Him was the chastisement
that brought us peace,
   and with His stripes we are healed.

All we like sheep have gone astray;
   we have turned every one
   to his own way;
and the LORD has laid on Him
   the iniquity of us all.

He was oppressed, and He was afflicted,
   yet He opened not His mouth;
like a lamb that is led to the slaughter,
   and like a sheep that before
   its shearers is silent,
   so He opened not His mouth.

By oppression and judgment He
was taken away;
   and as for His generation,
   who considered
that He was cut off out of the
land of the living,
   stricken for the transgression
   of My people?

And they made His grave
with the wicked
   and with a rich man in His death,

although He had done no violence,
   and there was no deceit
   in His mouth.

Yet it was the will of the LORD
to crush Him;
   He has put Him to grief;
when His soul makes an
offering for sin,
   He shall see His offspring;
   He shall prolong His days;
the will of the LORD shall prosper
in His hand.

Out of the anguish of His soul
   He shall see and be satisfied;
by His knowledge shall the righteous one,
My servant,
   make many to be accounted righteous,
   and He shall bear their iniquities.

Therefore I will divide Him a portion
with the many,
   and He shall divide the spoil
   with the strong,
because He poured out His
soul to death
   and was numbered with
   the transgressors;
yet He bore the sin of many,
   and makes intercession for the
   transgressors.

Isaiah 52:13–53:12

As you pray this prayer, remember that God looks graciously on you as part of His family because Christ was willing to be delivered up to death on the cross.

Almighty God, graciously behold this Your family for whom our Lord Jesus Christ was willing to be betrayed and delivered into the hands of sinful men to suffer death upon the cross; through the same Jesus Christ, Your Son, our Lord, who lives and reigns with You and the Holy Spirit, one God, now and forever. Amen.

Jesus' Death by Crucifixion

Crucifixion was horrifically painful. While hanging on the cross, the victim's full weight was borne by his wrists and feet at the point at which the spikes had been driven through them and into the wood. The greatest impact of crucifixion was on the victim's breathing. When "breathing in," a person normally activates the muscles of the chest and the diaphragm to bring air into the lungs. During exhalation, or "breathing out," a person relaxes the chest muscles and diaphragm and air moves out of the lungs. During crucifixion, this process is essentially reversed. The position of the body on the cross creates an emphysematous, or "barrel-chested," victim, preventing normal airflow in and out of the lungs.

Muscle contractions and the weight of the body as it hung on the cross forced the victim's chest into full expansion, the normal position of inspiration or breathing in. This created extreme difficulty with exhalation or breathing out. As a result, the victim was forced to breathe at the upper limits of lung expansion by taking shallow, rapid breaths. In the "normal" cross position, the weight of the victim's body created a barrel-chested shape that automatically pulled air into the lungs. For the victim to breathe out, he would have to push himself up into a more regular chest position, allowing the air to move out of his lungs. This could only be accomplished by rotating his nailed wrists and pushing up on his nail-driven feet. As fatigue set in, breathing took longer and became increasingly difficult.

Hold your arms out and up from your body as though they are anchored to a cross. Imagine your arms pulled upward as your body sags from its own weight. Feel your chest fill to capacity with air, then try to breathe out. Imagine repeating this process as you become increasingly unable to move your arms and legs.

Jesus' twisted torso and extended arms in this painting by Hendrik Terbrugghen shows the impact of crucifixion on Jesus' chest and the challenge breathing would have posed for Him. The impact is clear: an emaciated rib cage and stomach and skin that appears gangrenous. There can be no doubt: true worship of God is worship of Christ crucified.

To breathe in and out, Jesus would have to move up and down on the *stipes*. He would have to lift Himself up by pulling on His wrists and pushing up on His feet. With any movement, the spikes driven through His feet would have sent shearing pain up both legs. Likewise, with the movement upward to exhale, His arms would have rotated around the spikes, causing excruciating pain to shoot through His upper body and arms. It is difficult to imagine the agonizing pain. Each breath would have forced Jesus to push up on His feet, push His back against the *stipes*, and rotate His arms on the *patibulum*. His back, with its shredded flesh and muscle, would have grated against the rough timber. With each breath, each movement against the cross would have caused excruciating pain throughout the body and pushed the thorns ever deeper into His scalp. Jesus eventually would have tired of holding Himself in the fully extended breathing position and would have sagged into the crucified position. Yet to breathe, Jesus would have to repeat this agonizing process. Exhaustion soon followed.

In his comments on Isaiah 53:7 ("He was oppressed, and He was afflicted, yet He opened not His mouth; like a lamb that is led to the slaughter, and like a sheep that before its shearers is silent, so He opened not His mouth"), Martin Luther notes that when Jesus spoke on the cross, He spoke not out of vengeance and anger, but out of mercy and grace.

The prophet here points out how Christ suffered, that is, how patiently, never even uttering a word of complaint. St. Peter points this out (1 Peter 2:23): "Who, when he was reviled, reviled not again; when he suffered, he threatened not; but committed himself to him that judgeth righteously." Here the apostle points out the meaning of the words, "he opened not his mouth." Not that Christ did not speak during his suffering, for the passion account tells how on the cross he prayed to his heavenly Father and also spoke with his mother, Mary, and his disciple John. But he did not scold, did not curse, did not threaten, nor say, Watch out . . . you are going to be paid back. He did not seek revenge, nor did he say, Father, punish those who crucified, ridiculed, and despised me. But he suffered like a sheep which does not cry out against its shearer. Swine and other animals squeal and bellow, but a sheep does not cry out or curse its butcher or shearer. Christ's suffering was excruciatingly great and severe, so that he had every reason to complain and threaten, but he neither complained nor threatened, reasonable though it might have been for him to do so. But here there are only words of patience, compassion, benevolence, love, and gentleness; there is no evidence of anger, impatience, or revenge.

With heartfelt willingness he suffered for our sake, wishing no retribution, harboring no feelings of revenge. It is as the prophet said, "So he opened not his mouth."

The Gospels indicate that Jesus spoke at least seven times while hanging on the cross. Normally a person talks when exhaling or breathing out. A person can make words while breathing in, but such words are forced and difficult to understand.

As one would expect given Jesus' physical constraints and progressive fatigue, His last words were spoken in short phrases. To speak, Jesus had to push up on His feet, pull up on His wrists, and scrape His back on the *stipes*. This agonizing process was repeated seven times before He died.

The seven last words of Jesus show Him to be the ultimate teacher of salvation. His last words point to His death and resurrection as the way of salvation. For those who heard His words, Jesus showed how to love in the face of hatred, how to forgive in the process of being wrongfully punished, how to value one another and bind the human family together in God, and how to trust in God and be certain of life in heaven with the Father following death.

If one believes in Jesus Christ and trusts in the power of His death and resurrection, that person will drink from Jesus' cup of eternal salvation. Each of Jesus' words from the cross uniquely points to His suffering and death as the way of salvation.

In this fresco attributed to Parri Spinello, the emaciation of Christ's body and the positioning of his torso emphasizes the agony He underwent to breathe while hanging on the cross. Even Mary and the beloved disciple, John, appear to turn their faces away from this man of sorrow, broken by the wasted wood of the tree of the cross.

This painted cross from the thirteenth century denotes the forgiving heart of Jesus. Bonaventura Berlinghieri depicts Christ's victory on the cross as being for your good, a victory that wins forgiveness for sinners. Mary, the epitome of the Christian life of faith, is pointing at her Son and the mercy of His cross. At each of the four ends of the cross's beams are the images of the four Evanglists, representing the proclamation of the Good News of the cross to the four corners of the earth.

The physiology of dysfunctional respiratory activity and congestive heart failure—compounded by extreme fatigue, hypovolemia (low body fluid), severe anemia, electrolyte abnormalities, and subsequent kidney failure—contributed to a cascade of life-ending changes in Christ's normal bodily functions.

How did Jesus' crucifixion lead to congestive heart failure? The pulling of the chest into full expansion for a prolonged period of time would have led to a disruption of normal respiratory activity and gas exchange in the alveoli (small air sacks) of the lungs. Disruption of the exchange of carbon dioxide with oxygen in the alveoli leads to a buildup of carbon dioxide (hypercapnia) and a decrease of oxygen (hypoxemia), which is called acute alveolar hypoventilation. This means that body metabolism is producing more carbon dioxide than the lungs can clear out by ventilation.

As a result of this accumulation of carbon dioxide and lack of oxygen exchange, life-threatening metabolic changes take place in the body. The development of acute hypercapnia and hypoxemia leads quickly to a change in the acid level of the body fluids (acidosis). The triad of carbon dioxide buildup, oxygen loss, and increased acidity in body fluids leads to constriction of the heart's (pulmonary) resistance vessels. This makes it harder for blood to flow from the right side of the heart to the lungs (acute pulmonary artery congestion). The increased resistance to the flow of blood into the lungs puts more pressure on the right ventricle and right atrium of the heart and contributes to congestive heart failure on the right side. The overexpansion of the right ventricle, the stretching of the pericardial sack around the heart, and the spasm of the remaining bronchial smooth muscles in the lungs is a life-threatening state of congestive heart failure.

"Father, forgive them, for they know not what they do." In the greatest miracle of all, Jesus asks His Father to forgive the people who crucified Him because they did not know what they were doing. Jesus died in the manner in which He lived. He preached and practiced forgiveness and turning the other cheek. What power was demonstrated while He was hanging on the cross! Even as His body is destroyed, He forgives those who have destroyed it. Here is forgiveness for all—all who deny the true God who comes to have mercy.

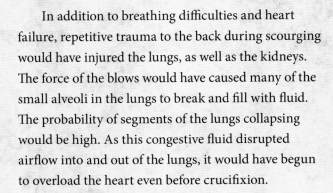

"Truly, I say to you, today you will be with Me in paradise." As Jesus listened to the two men hanging on crosses next to Him, one man mocked Him and offered a challenge: save Yourself and us!

If Jesus had removed Himself from the cross in response to the challenge, the man would have been an instant convert. But that would not have been faith in the true God, who comes with mercy even for those who crucify Him.

Instead, Christ had mercy and gave comfort and a promise to the other condemned man, who had showed compassion to the one suffering beside him. Jesus promised this repentant thief that he would be with Him that day in paradise.

Paradise is the promise of the merciful God to all who are in the throes of death. In the words of the sixth-century theologian Romanos:

The Devil speaks:
Now then, Hades, mourn and I join in unison with you in wailing. Let us lament as we see the tree which we planted Changed into a holy trunk. Robbers, murderers, tax gatherers, harlots, Rest beneath it, and make nests In its branches in order that they might gather The fruit of sweetness from the supposedly sterile wood. For they cling to the cross as the tree of life.

In addition to breathing difficulties and heart failure, repetitive trauma to the back during scourging would have injured the lungs, as well as the kidneys. The force of the blows would have caused many of the small alveoli in the lungs to break and fill with fluid. The probability of segments of the lungs collapsing would be high. As this congestive fluid disrupted airflow into and out of the lungs, it would have begun to overload the heart even before crucifixion.

One of the primary functions of the lungs, besides the exchange of carbon dioxide for oxygen, is to work in conjunction with the kidneys to tightly regulate the body's acid-base levels. Another complication of hypercapnia (high carbon dioxide levels) and hypoxia (low oxygen levels) is the progression to a high level of acid in body fluids (severe acidosis). Changes in the body's acid level can contribute to kidney failure, worsening the probability for lung failure. Either the lungs or the kidneys must compensate for the other if one is overloaded or damaged. During the process of crucifixion, both systems are overloaded and neither can compensate adequately.

Subsequent common complications of the buildup of carbon dioxide include (1) cardiac arrhythmias or irregular beating patterns of the heart, which often are life threatening; (2) bronchial obstruction from the lack of clearance and thickening of bronchial lung secretions; (3) pneumothorax or collapse of segments of remaining good lung tissue; and (4) acute right- and/ or left-side heart failure and the inability to circulate blood throughout the rest of the body and its organs.

Notice Giovanni Antonio Pordenone's use of blue, a color of royalty. While the blue of the Roman emperor and the empire appear to hold sway, it is Christ robed in blue and bleeding purple who is the anointed King. This is His coronation, though the kingdom of God is not of this world. Amid this chaotic scene on Golgotha, Pordenone focuses on the believing thief (left) and Jesus. Having heard Jesus' word of salvation and life after death, the repentant thief leans toward his Savior. Amid death, and as the unbelieving thief is bound to the cross, life reigns through the forgiving word and promise of Jesus, "Today you will be with Me in Paradise" (Luke 23:43).

Michelangelo's famous *Pieta* depicts the devotion of a still youthful Mary. With tender affection, she cradles her Son in her lap. Even as in the midst of His agony Jesus treasured Mary and entrusted His mother to the disciple John, so Mary continues to treasure the Word, holding her Son in her arms and in her heart.

Kidney failure also would have been a likely physiological effect of Jesus' suffering and crucifixion. During the scourging, Jesus would have suffered repetitive trauma to His back, which would have been as damaging to the kidneys as to the lungs. Like the lungs, the kidneys are protected by the muscles of the back and the posterior ribs. This area would have been the focal point of the trauma caused by the metal balls on the *flagrum*. This trauma would cause swelling (edema), along with subsequent inflammation in both the lungs and kidneys. This swelling, bleeding, and inflammation would disrupt the normal function of Jesus' kidneys and His lungs. Disruption of normal blood flow into and out of the kidneys would result in acute kidney failure, thus altering many of the body's mineral and electrolyte levels. Any single change, but especially the combination of electrolyte changes, is life threatening.

All these changes would become more critical in light of Jesus' severe dehydration. The lungs work with the kidneys to regulate the electrolytes and gases of the body. Trauma to both systems, along with electrolyte imbalances and the lack of oxygen, placed Jesus in a life-threatening state following His scourging.

"Woman, behold, your son. . . . Behold, your mother." One of Jesus' last words from the cross demonstrated mercy to His mother, who was enduring the agony of witnessing the terrible abuse of her Son. Jesus provided for His mother's earthly care and blessed the bond between mother and son when He placed her in the care of His disciple John.

In hearing and remembering Jesus' death on the cross for us—especially as we gather in worship around the cross—we, like the beloved disciple and Mary, take our place at the foot of the cross and pray:

Lord Jesus Christ, as we kneel at the foot of your cross, help us to see and know your love for us, so that we may place at your feet all that we have and are. Crucified Savior, naked God, you hang disgraced and powerless. Grieving, we dare to hope, as we wait at the cross with your mother and friend. Amen.

Anemia would have contributed to Jesus' deteriorating physical state. During His Passion, Jesus was subjected to physical abuse. He was repeatedly beaten in the face and head. His scalp was punctured by multiple thorns. The muscles and flesh on His back were shredded and left gaping and bleeding. There would have been a continuous loss of blood from the nail holes in His feet and wrists.

The emotional suffering Jesus' endured in the Garden of Gethsemane led to extreme perspiration and hemohidrosis. Likewise, excessive sweating (severe diaphoresis) is a documented phenomenon during crucifixion. The continuous, though slow, blood loss, coupled with ongoing body fluid loss, would have contributed over time to a state of profound anemia and contributed to Jesus' overall state of dehydration. The continuous blood loss would have contributed to the fatigue that was apparent as He made His way to Golgotha.

Because the cross is the mercy of God to sinners, we can take comfort even as we consider that Christ bled for us. So Johann Sebastian Bach proclaims in the St. John Passion:

In the bottom of my heart, your name and cross alone shines forth every age and hour, for which I can be joyful. Appear before me in the image, as comfort in my distress: how you, Lord Christ, so abundantly did bleed to death!

Albrecht Dürer's engraving shows a physically strong and vital Jesus, yet a Man crucified for the salvation of the world. His death is the death of the old Adam and of death itself, signified by the skull of Adam at the foot of the cross. Jesus' life is life itself and the life of the new Adam: "For as in Adam all die, so also in Christ shall all be made alive" (1 Corinthians 15:22).

Tradition has it that in this city, in fact, on this very spot, Adam lived and died. The place where our Lord was crucified is called Calvary, because the skull of the first man was buried there. So it came to pass that the blood of the second Adam, that is, the blood of Christ, as it dropped from the cross, washed away the sins of the buried one who was first formed, the first Adam, and thus the words of the apostle were fulfilled: "Awake, you who sleep, and arise from the dead, and Christ shall give you light" [Ephesians 5:14].

—*Jerome*

Jesus' dying words were sounded forth like the triumphant shouts of a victorious army. He was dying not because He must, but because He would. He had said: "For this reason the Father loves Me, because I lay down My life that I may take it up again. No one takes it from Me, but I lay it down of My own accord. I have authority to lay it down, and I have authority to take it up again. This charge I have received from My Father" (John 10:17–18). Therefore Jesus cried out to His Father with a loud voice: "Father, into Your hands I commit My spirit!" (Luke 23:46). As He breathed His last, Jesus delivered to His Father that precious soul that had purchased for sin-cursed and death-doomed men deliverance, freedom from the curse and guilt of sin, freedom from the horror of the grave and the clutches of death. Jesus gave Himself, His life, His soul for man's redemption.

Another severe complication of the electrolyte imbalance caused by water loss, blood loss, fatigue, and lung and kidney malfunctions is the inevitable development of severe contraction of the muscles (tetany). Violent whole body contractions and severe muscle cramps would have been pulled Jesus' arms and legs against the restraining nails. Jesus' inability to move His arms or legs, intensified by the gradual buildup of carbonic acid in His muscles and circulatory system, would have intensified the pain because carbonic acid increases muscle excitation and intensifies the muscle contraction.

The cramps and searing pain would have started in Jesus' forearms where the spikes were driven through the median nerves. The constriction and pain would have progressed up both arms to His shoulders and neck. The large muscles on each side and in the front of the neck (sternocleidomastoid muscles)—which are used to turn, flex, and extend the head—would have been forced by the restraint of His body into a position in which the head is pulled down (emprosthotonic). However, when Jesus pushed up on His feet to exhale, His head would have been forced into a backward position (opisthotonic position). In addition, the chest muscles (pectoralis), along with the neck muscles and the large diaphragm muscle (all used for inhalation), would have been pulled into an upward, tightened, and contracted position while the weight of the body pulled in the opposite direction. As a result, the abdominal muscles would have been pulled into full contraction, giving a concave appearance to the abdominal wall.

As with the arms, so also the knees would have been bent or flexed to be nailed to the front of the *stipes*. Pain and contraction would have started at the feet just like at the wrists. This intense pain would have spread up the large leg muscles. The full contraction of the calf and thigh muscles would have been excruciating. Consider the pain of a charley horse or leg cramp coupled with the inability to straighten out the leg to relieve the pain.

The liturgical context in which the benefits of Christ's crucifixion are received comes to the forefront in this painting by Rogier van der Weyden. The red cloth hangs like a parament from an altar, denoting the blood that is poured from the cross into the mouths of believers at the Lord's Supper. The devotion of Mary and John at the cross models the faith-filled devotion of the baptized children of God. Faith finds its focus in the blood poured out for the life of the world.

"Eloi, Eloi, lama sabacthani," which means, "My God, My God, why have You forsaken Me?"

This cry of suffering and dereliction comes from the One who heard and trusted the word of His Father that He was the beloved Son. Now Jesus is dying, hung on the cross by the world's unmerciful hands. Those who hear His cry know that life and salvation come only through suffering and death, especially the suffering of abandonment by God. Walter Wangerin Jr.'s description of Jesus' final hours manifest the agony of the cross.

It is noon. And now, when the flashes of lightning themselves are extinguished, the earth is utterly black. Darkness an hour—while the fierce wind makes the rain sting like sand on the skin, and no one, no one exists in all the world but Jesus and his wretched body. If he should call out, who would hear? The wind pulls and snaps his hair like a banner.

All his wounds have tongues. They are screaming in pitches higher than hearing.

Darkness another hour—darkness, coiled and thick, itself a power entoiling him, binding his chest and his heart and his mind. Jesus can neither think nor breathe. He is sunk down in tehom, the great engulfing flood of the dead, the deeps that boil beneath creation. He has been swallowed by chaos. This is the place: it is here that he is dying.

Darkness the third hour—and now he knows obliteration. Jesus has been blotted out of the Book of Life. Not even God is here.

"Eli?"

No, not even his Father, whose will he is even now obeying, the Father who has loved him from the beginning, whom he has loved, whom he has called Abba.

"Eli? Eli?"

Where is his Father now? Has the Son become so foul that even God cannot look upon him?

It is Jesus of Nazareth who howls out of Sheol. None but him. He can hear the words. They are his own words. He howls them up to heaven:

"My God!" He shrieks. "My God, why have you forsaken me?"

Silence.

The universe is silenced by that cry.

Jesus throws his body outward from the cross. His ribs splay apart in the straining. His shoulders form hollows at the pits of his neck. His mouth is an empty canyon.

Someone says, "Was he calling Elijah?"

"I don't know," says someone else. "Wait and see."

A third person is running through the darkness toward the crosses.

Jesus allows his body to droop. The weight of it draws out his arms, closing the cage around his lungs, constricting his breathing. He can breathe only in faint pants. But he whispers, "I'm thirsty."

"Yes! Yes!" cries the person who has been running toward him. "Yes, drink this." On a long stalk, this most civil individual raises a sponge to Jesus' lips. He sucks and tastes a common wine. He drinks. Jesus has never drunk so sweet a drink in all his life before.

The rain has ended. The wind has died. A little light sifts down like flour from the clouds.

"It is finished," Jesus gasps. "Father. Into your hands I commend my spirit."

His body falls far forward. His head sinks down between the wings of his rising arms. His heavy black hair, his long wet hair falls over his head like a curtain. An everlasting sigh issues from his open mouth, and that is the end. He dies.

Mathias Gruenewald's graphic presentation of the crucifixion expresses well Christ's suffering. The blood flows from the pores of His body, and the severely distended hands and fingers communicate the severity of His agony. Yet as John the Baptist's pointing finger indicates, as well as the lamb at his feet, this is not the Father's final word, because Jesus is the Lamb of God who takes away the sin of the world.

143

In a feeble attempt to temporarily relieve the severe muscle cramps and progressive reversal of normal heart and kidney function, Jesus would have tried to restore His breathing to a more normal pattern, thus realigning the blood flow in His extremities. In an effort to exhale the life-draining carbon dioxide and inhale fresh life-saving oxygen, Jesus would have pushed up on His feet, rotated His arms around the squared nails, and pulled His body up on the cross. From the spikes, shearing pain would have shot up both legs with any movement. The rotation of the arms around the spikes would have caused lightening-like pain through His arms and entire upper body. Each breath would have forced Jesus to push up on His feet, push His back against the *stipes*, and rotate His arms on the *patibulum*. The open sores and the torn flesh and muscle on His back would have grated against the rough timber. Each movement up and down with each breath would have caused excruciating pain over Jesus' back, arms, legs, and head, the crown of thorns pushing ever deeper into His flesh. Jesus eventually would have tired of holding Himself in this position, only to sag back down into the crucified, life-ending position.

To continue breathing, Jesus would need to repeat this agonizing, painful, and life-draining process. The crucifixion was spent straightening out His body to exhale, and then slumping down again to inhale. The result was an alternation between attempting to breathe normally and progressive asphyxia. Exhaustion was soon to follow. The only positive in death would have been the cessation of the pain.

It is the slouched position of extreme exhaustion that Bernard of Clairvaux had in mind when he wrote "O Sacred Head, Now Wounded."

O sacred Head, now wounded,
With grief and shame weighed down,
Now scornfully surrounded
With thorns, Thine only crown.
O sacred Head, what glory,
What bliss, till now was Thine!
Yet, though despised and gory,
I joy to call Thee mine.

How pale Thou art with anguish,
With sore abuse and scorn!
How doth Thy face now languish
That once was bright as morn!
Grim death, with cruel rigor,
Hath robbed Thee of Thy life;
Thus Thou hast lost Thy vigor,
Thy strength, in this sad strife.

Even as Jesus' ribs reveal His effort to breathe, He cannot hold Himself up, and His body sags down into death. Carlo Crivelli's painting captures well the effects of Christ's Passion as expressed in Bernard of Clairvaux's poem "O Sacred Head, Now Wounded."

"I thirst." Jesus called out that He was thirsty. In the fullness of His suffering as the incarnate Son of God, He proclaimed the depth of His pain: He was parched to the bone. He had been deprived of the water that sustains life, which He as the Word of God had called into being.

While drinking the cup of death on the cross, Jesus was preparing the cup of salvation for those who would believe in Him. Jesus thirsted for life on earth, so He drank the bitter wine offered to Him. Yet He was ready to drink the cup of His Father, the cup of life that His Father had promised and that He would drink in the kingdom of His Father.

In drinking the cup of suffering and death, Jesus pours out for you the cup of eternal life that flows from His side. "Whoever feeds on My flesh and drinks My blood has eternal life, and I will raise him up on the last day" (John 6:54).

Hieronymus Wierix produced this engraving entitled *Christ in the Wine Press*, which was well-received in Catholic Europe during the 1600s. The engraving demonstrates both the work of redemption on our behalf and Christ's institution of the Lord's Supper. In the background, Wierix includes the Old Testament patriarchs and judges, depicting them planting grape vines, from which the apostles (in the foreground) are harvesting the fruit. But "instead of the grapes, it is Christ who will be crushed. His cross has been transformed into the press and God the Father and the dove of the Holy Spirit bear down on the cross to effect the sacrifice. The inscription on the print quotes the verse from Isaiah which is the basis of the imagery: 'I have trodden the winepress alone; and of the people there was none with me' (Isaiah 63:3). Christ's blood fills a chalice held by two angels, and on the right in the background, the Virgin contemplates her son's fate, her heart pierced by a sword. On the left, sinners are seen praying in preparation for receiving the Eucharist."

The cross is the end of life for sinful man and the fallen creation, and it is the beginning of life for the new man and the new creation. Clement of Alexandria rejoices in the cross as creation renewed.
Sunset to sunrise changes now,
For God creates the world anew;
On the Redeemer's thorn-crowned brow The wonders of that dawn we view. Although the sun withholds its light Yet a more heav'nly lamp shines here; And from the cross on Calv'ry's height Gleams of eternity appear. Here in o'erwhelming final strife The Lord of life has victory; And sin is slain, and death brings life, and earth inherits heaven's key.

The devotion and affection of Mary, the women, Joseph of Arimathea (on the ladder), Nicodemus (removing the nails), and John (holding Jesus' legs) is conveyed by the tenderness with which Jesus' body is removed from the cross. Duccio di Buoninsegna depicts the emotion of the moment as Mary kisses her Son's face and Mary Magdalene caresses Jesus' arm.

The Proof and Cause of Jesus' Death

The removal of the body from the cross and burial was generally granted at the request of the family, in accord with Roman practice. Before the body could be removed, the Roman centurion in charge of the crucifixion detail needed to complete his duties by certifying that the victim was truly dead.

If the crucified victim was still clinging to life, the centurion could choose between two methods to complete the process of dying. The first method was to break the legs of the individual. This process was called *crurifragium* or *skelokopia*. The legs were beaten with a club typically carried by the soldiers. The bones in the lower legs could be easily broken with solid blows across the legs. At about three feet from the ground, the lower legs were an easy target for an effortless swing, not unlike a baseball swing. If the shock from breaking the bones in the legs did not kill the victim immediately, the culmination of the entire process would guarantee death in a few minutes. Breaking the legs prevented the victim from pushing up on his feet to exhale, leading to asphyxiation within a short period of time.

The Holy Spirit had called other people for this, namely, Joseph and Nicodemus. They were inspired with courage and bravery: Joseph, petitioning Pilate for the body of Christ; Nicodemus, arranging for the burial. They were disciples empowered by Christ's suffering. Before they had been anxious and frightened; now they are confident and courageous. Christ's sacrifice and prayers on the cross penetrate and bear fruit. The thief at Christ's right was the first fruit of Christ's death; Joseph and Nicodemus, the second. They, like the thief, became courageous. Joseph went to Pilate to ask for the body of Christ; Nicodemus brought an hundred pound weight of myrrh and aloes. Once they were secret disciples of Christ for fear of the Jews; now, they are his disciples and confessors openly.

These were men of power and influence. Joseph hailed from Arimathea and was a wealthy man, an esteemed official in Jerusalem. Nicodemus was a Pharisee and a member of the Sanhedrin. Thus in that very hostile crowd of high priests, scribes, Pharisees, elders, and people in general, Christ at his death finds two gallant men to claim his body that hangs disgracefully on the cross, and to give it burial most honorably, discounting all risk to life and limb, to earthly possessions and reputation. Now they have greater faith, confidence, and courage than when the Lord was alive, so great is the fruit and power of the suffering and death of Christ.

—*Martin Luther*

Hallgrimur Petursson's poem *Jesus' Wounded Side*, while not directly referring to the Lord's Supper, rejoices in the saving benefits bestowed by the flow of Jesus' blood.

At even a soldier, hard, unfeeling, Approached the cross, his deed to do: His spear, the Savior's side unsealing, In hate that loving heart pierced through: Water and blood forth flowed, down stealing: Prophets that mystic stream foreknew. God wrought for man, His love forth-showing, When Moses smote the rock of old; And lo! Through Israel's camp on-flowing, Out brake the longed-for flood, and rolled, New strength, new joy, new life bestowing, On lips that quaffed it, pure and cold. God wrought for man, mankind redeeming, When Christ was pierced by roman spear, And o'er the thirsty world down-streaming, Forth gushed a fountain, cool and clear, Till souls, beside those waters gleaming, Forgot in joy sin's desert drear. Beside that well for aye abiding, New strength, new joy, new life I gain; Within that cleft securely hiding, No care can mark, no sorrow stain; Here rests the blissful soul confiding, Here faith the healing draught can drain. Lord, let my heart, this gift receiving, Beat one glad anthem, to Thy praise; And may the stream, thy pierced heart leaving, Refresh and heal me all my days: Thus, by thy blood my life retrieving, A psalm of endless thanks I'll raise. For, through that pierced heart up gazing, Mine eyes all heaven's expanses see; The glory of that love amazing, Enthralled, I scan unceasingly, Until my soul's dark night greets, praising, The dawn of God's eternity.

The second method of assuring death involved a Roman soldier thrusting his spear into the victim's chest cavity. This "death thrust" maneuver penetrated the lungs, the sacs that surround the lungs (pleura), the heart (pericardium), and the chambers of the heart.

Roman foot soldiers were professional fighters who had battled and conquered much of the then-known world, and the spear was their weapon of choice. The short spear was approximately four feet long and consisted of a three-foot wooden shaft and one-foot metal tip. A longer version (approximately six feet long) may have been carried by the centurion. The "death thrust" through the chest and into the heart by either the short or long spear would have been taught to the soldiers as a standard offensive maneuver. The spear would have been held in one hand at the lower third of the shaft, and with a smooth, lunging motion, the arm would have been extended toward the victim. The spear would have entered just below or at the right lower ribs and traveled through the right lung and diaphragm. The tip would have passed through the heart sack, already stretched with pericardial fluid, and entered the right ventricle, which also would have been stretched to capacity from congestive heart failure. A swoosh of air leaking out of the penetrated chest cavity may have been heard, or this may have been blocked by pulmonary fluid congested in the lower portion of the thorax. As the spear passed through the pericardial sack, thin, watery fluid would have leaked. The passage of the spear tip into the heart muscle itself, as well as into the chamber filled with blood, would have resulted in a gush of blood down the spear tip and through the hole made in the chest and abdomen.

Note the angels who are holding chalices and catching the blood that flowed from Jesus' wounds. Thus the artist visualizes the benefits of Christ's death, which He proclaimed in the words He spoke to institute the Lord's Supper, "Given and shed for you for the forgiveness of sins." The forgiveness, life, and salvation obtained for us by Jesus' death and resurrection are delivered to us through His broken body given to us and His blood poured into our mouths in His blessed Meal, as Martin Luther reminds us:

As His pledge of love undying,
He, this precious food
supplying,
Gives His body with the bread,
And with the wine the blood
He shed.

Praise the Father, who from
heaven
To His own this food has given,
Who, to mend what we have
done,
Gave into death His only Son.

151

The other gospels mark Jesus' death with miraculous signs in the ambiance: The Temple curtain is torn; tombs open and bodies of the saints come forth; and an expression of faith is evoked from a Roman centurion. But the Fourth Gospel localizes the sign in the body of Jesus itself: When the side of Jesus is pierced, there comes forth blood and water. In [John] 7:38-39 we heard: "From within him shall flow rivers of living water," with the explanation that the water symbolized the Spirit which would be given when Jesus had been glorified. That is now fulfilled, for the admixture of blood to the water is the sign that Jesus has passed from this world to the Father and has been glorified. It is not impossible that the fourth evangelist intends here a reference not only to the gift of the Spirit but also to the two channels (baptism and the eucharist) through which the Spirit had been communicated to the believers of his own community, with water signifying baptism, and blood the eucharist.

—*Raymond E. Brown*

Questions center around the blood and water mixture that flowed from Jesus' heart and the order in which they are mentioned in the Gospels. The blood, which is mentioned first, would have come from the right ventricle after it was pierced by the spear. This ventricle would have been under a great deal of pressure from the congestive changes that had taken place while Jesus was hanging on the cross. The watery fluid would have come from the pericardial sack surrounding the heart. This would have been thinner than the blood but would have flowed more slowly, because it was under less pressure when released. The quantity of fluid around the heart would have been considerably less than the amount of blood contained inside the right chamber; thus it would have been mentioned after the greater amount of blood that flowed.

With the thrust of the spear, all human attempts to create life apart from God are ended. The only life humankind now can have is the life that God gives, as stated in the second stanza of the hymn "The Royal Banners Forward Go."

Where deep for us
the spear was dyed,
Life's torrent rushing
from His side,
To wash us in
the precious flood
Where flowed the water
and the blood.

Drinking the chalice of Jesus' blood in the Lord's Supper enabled Christian martyrs to shed their blood as their Savior did, a death that Polycarp of Smyrna referred to in this way:

God of the . . . whole race of the just who live in your presence: I bless you because you have judged me worthy of this day and of this hour; worthy to be added to the number of the martyrs; worthy to *drink the chalice of your Christ,* so as to rise up to eternal life in body and soul in the immortality of the Holy Spirit.

While a lamb bound as an offering is common in depictions of the incarnation, Francisco de Zurbaran instead depicts the solitary figure of a lamb bound for slaughter on an altar slab. Christ, the Lamb of God, in humility, innocence, and purity, through His sacrificial death on the altar of the cross, has brought to fulfillment Israel's sacrificial system of mercy. Where "the offering of the body of Jesus Christ once for all" (Hebrews 10:10) is received by faith, there all sins have been forgiven. "There is no longer any offering for sin" (Hebrews 10:18).

153

Prominent in this painting by Maerten van Heemskerck is the thrust of the spear into Jesus' side, the final assault of death on the One who is Life itself. Other aspects of the crucifixion are also apparent: the darkness of the sky at Jesus' death, the sponge soaked in vinegar raised to Jesus' lips, the overturned bucket of vinegar and gall, the soldiers gambling for Jesus' tunic, and the skull of Adam at the foot of the cross. Each element reveals Golgotha as the place of death, yet at this place Christ overcame the curse of sin and death for us.

The "death thrust" would not have been more painful than the other terrible things that had been experienced while being crucified. It would have given quick and certain death to the victim and would have been, at least in relation to the suffering, a welcome relief. The death thrust certified death and was performed on any victim before the body could be taken down and buried.

The centurion would have known Jesus' body was requested for burial and would have certified His death in this usual manner. The biblical accounts proclaim that Jesus did indeed receive a spear wound through the right side of His chest. It is this blow to Jesus' heart that allowed His followers and mother to remove His body from the cross and prepare it for burial.

The Shroud of Turin shows an oblique, almost horizontal, delivery of a lance to the body imposed on the cloth. If Jesus hung on a *tau* cross, the centurion's spear easily would have penetrated the right side of Jesus' body and entered His heart at just short of a horizontal trajectory. The blow was a natural and "kind" gesture that certified death.

"It is finished."

The last words of Jesus were simple. All that had been prophesied had come to pass. All He could do was done. Jesus had completed the task given Him by the Father. The Son of God had lived as fully man. He had been hated but showed love and mercy, even to those who crucified Him. He had been abused but healed others. He had been wronged but showed forgiveness. He had come into the darkness to bring light. Now Jesus was ready to go home to His Father on the spirit-filled wings of the Father's promise.

"Father, into Your hands I commit My spirit." Despite complete agony, Jesus does not despair. He trusts in His Father's promise and places Himself into His Father's hands. In the Garden of Gethsemane, Jesus entrusted His earthly body to God, His Father. Now in His last moments on earth, Jesus commends His spirit to His Father. He knew the way back to His Father: to trust in His Father and His life-giving word of promise. Jesus' work of redemption was complete, and He was going home. This is the prayer of all who trust in the Father through Christ.

It can be certain that Jesus died while He hung on the cross. Even if the removal of His body prior to death had been possible, as some critics believe, it is doubtful that Jesus could have been revived and death prevented, even if the resuscitation attempt had taken place in the trauma unit of a modern hospital. Jesus' body had been destroyed beyond repair or renewal. Indeed, when He offered up a loud cry and bowed His head, Jesus undoubtedly was dead.

As He acknowledged in the Garden of Gethsemane with His resolve to undergo this ordeal, Jesus entrusted Himself to the hands of His Father, sacrificed His human body, and died. The Roman soldiers and onlookers all recognized the moment of His death.

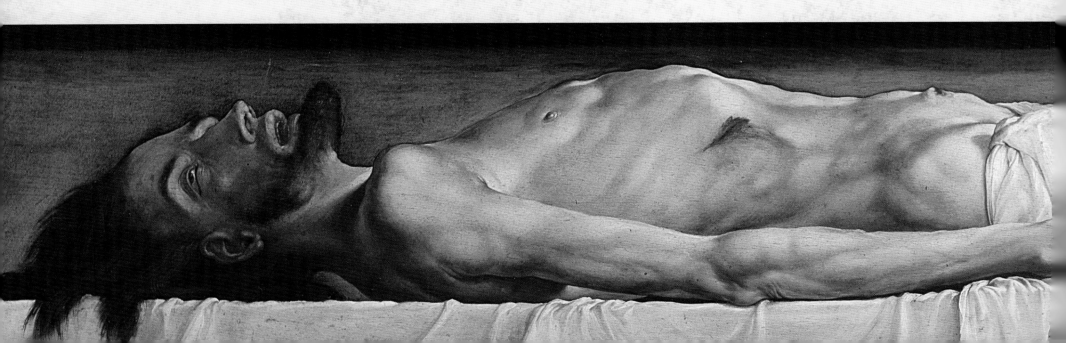

Jesus truly died on the cross. To claim anything else is to deny the will of God, the plan of salvation that Jesus came to fulfill. The Early Church theologian Adamantius clearly confesses the death of Jesus.

It was not in appearance only that he died. It was a true death. . . . The spirit did not expire since it was eternal and incorruptible. But there was one who had the spirit who indeed expired who, while expiring, commended the spirit to the Father. He is the one whom Joseph wrapped in the linen cloth and buried. He did not wrap up and bury a shadow but him who was nailed to the tree.

There can be no doubt that Jesus is flesh and blood and that death has pursued Him to the end in this painting by Hans Holbein the Younger. Our Savior's body is in a state of rigor mortis, His ribs protrude, His bones show through His skin, He has wasted away, the skin on His fingers and feet has begun to change color and decay, His eyes have rolled back in His head, and His fingers are curved in on themselves. Holbein's picture captures Isaiah's description of the Suffering Servant: "As one from whom men hide their faces He was despised, and we esteemed Him not" (Isaiah 53:3).

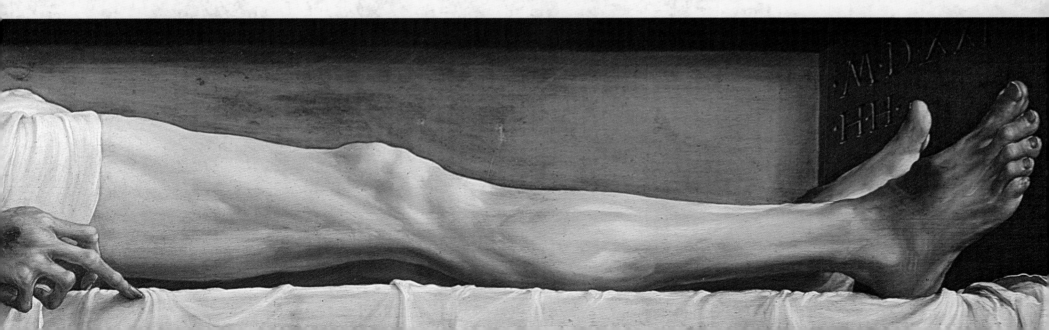

While Christ's death was part of the Father's plan, ultimately the cause of His death lies with rebellious humanity, as is made clear in these stanzas from the hymn "O Darkest Woe."

O sorrow dread!
Our God is dead,
Upon the cross extended.
There His love enlivened us
As His life was ended.

O child of woe:
Who struck the blow
That killed our gracious Master?
"It was I," thy conscience cries,
"I have wrought disaster!"

Thy Bridegroom dead!
God's Lamb has bled
Upon Thy sin forever,
Pouring out His sinless self
In this vast endeavor.

O Jesus Christ,
Who sacrificed
Thy life for lifeless mortals:
Be my life in death and bring
Me to heaven's portals!

Christ, the life of all the living,
Christ, the death of death, our foe,
Who, Thyself for me once giving
To the darkest depths of woe:
Through Thy suff'rings, death, and merit
I eternal life inherit.
Thousand, thousand thanks shall be,
Dearest Jesus, unto Thee.

Thou, ah! Thou, hast taken on Thee
Bonds and stripes, a cruel rod;
Pain and scorn were heaped upon Thee,
O Thou sinless Son of God!
Thus didst Thou my soul deliver
From the bonds of sin forever.
Thousand, thousand thanks shall be,
Dearest Jesus, unto Thee.

Thou hast borne the smiting only
That my wounds might all be whole;
Thou hast suffered, sad and lonely,
Rest to give my weary soul;
Yea, the curse of God enduring,
Blessing unto me securing.
Thousand, thousand thanks shall be,
Dearest Jesus, unto Thee.

Heartless scoffers did surround Thee,
Treating Thee with shameful scorn
And with piercing thorns they
    crowned Thee.
All disgrace Thou, Lord, hast borne,
That as Thine Thou mightest own me
And with heav'nly glory crown me.
Thousand, thousand thanks shall be,
Dearest Jesus, unto Thee.

Thou hast suffered men to bruise Thee,
That from pain I might be free;
Falsely did Thy foes accuse Thee:
Thence I gain security;

Comfortless Thy soul did languish
Me to comfort in my anguish.
Thousand, thousand thanks shall be,
Dearest Jesus, unto Thee.

Thou hast suffered great affliction
And hast borne it patiently,
Even death by crucifixion,
Fully to atone for me;
Thou didst choose to be tormented
That my doom should be prevented.
Thousand, thousand thanks shall be,
Dearest Jesus, unto Thee.

Then, for all that wrought my pardon,
For Thy sorrows deep and sore,
For Thine anguish in the Garden,
I will thank Thee evermore,
Thank Thee for Thy groaning, sighing,
For Thy bleeding and Thy dying,
For that last triumphant cry,
And shall praise Thee, Lord, on high.

It was Jesus' death and the manner of His death that led the centurion to confess that truly this man was the Son of God, the German words beneath Jesus' feet. The centurion recognized God and God's will in the death of Jesus, as depicted in this painting by Lucas Cranach the Elder. Since Cranach was the court painter for the three electors and rulers of Saxony during Luther's lifetime, the centurion may be modeled after them, especially John Frederick the Magnanimous, the elector in power when Cranach composed this painting. Since the centurion's confession was considered a preeminent example of justification by grace through faith alone in Christ, it would be natural to model him after the prince who most fervently embraced and furthered the central teaching of the Reformation: "People are freely justified for Christ's sake, through faith, when they believe that they are received into favor and that their sins are forgiven for Christ's sake. By His death, Christ made satisfaction for our sins. God counts this faith for righteousness in His sight (Romans 3 and 4 [3:21–26; 4:5])" (Augsburg Confession IV 2–3).

Reviewing the three main aspects of Christ's Passion in reverse order of occurrence may better illuminate the suffering that Jesus underwent for the forgiveness of our sins.

Today it is unthinkable that we would allow someone to be thrown onto his back to have nails driven through his wrists and feet.

We probably would not allow someone to rip the robe from Christ's scourged back, even if He were our most hated enemy.

Scourging—with its ripping of flesh and muscle—would make us turn away in disgust.

We would not tolerate placing a crown of thorns on Jesus' head or repeatedly hitting this crown with sticks.

Now that you have some knowledge of the process of crucifixion, imagine the pain and suffering Jesus experienced for you. Consider that in the garden Jesus not only foresaw what would happen but also experienced the agony. Thus Jesus asked to be spared from the physical and emotional destruction of His human body through this cruel, painful, and humiliating method of execution. In this very understandable request, we recognize that Jesus was truly human.

The actual cause of Jesus' death was most likely a combination of physiologic conditions. The most common theory regarding the cause of Christ's death was a combination of hypovolemic shock and exhaustion asphyxia. In other words, He had a low volume of body water and circulating blood (hypovolemic shock) combined with a concentration of carbon dioxide and a lack of oxygen in His body (exhaustion asphyxia). He entered hypovolemic shock because He had consumed no water for some time, had suffered an excessive loss of water from extreme perspiration, and had lost a tremendous amount of blood. Jesus had nothing to drink from the Last Supper until His death. No water intake for perhaps twenty-four hours surely contributed to the depletion of His total body fluids. Jesus perspired excessively in the Garden of Gethsemane and would have done so also during the crucifixion, contributing to the deficit of total body water. Excessive water and electrolyte loss from crucifixion has been well documented.

The brightness of the colors of the figures in Rosso Fiorentino's painting of Christ's descent from the cross contrasts with the dead body of the Savior. The effect of the crucifixion on the Son of God is vividly apparent. As attested by the gangrenous green color of His body, Jesus is definitely dead. The movement of life flows through the rest of the figures, with the exception of Mary, who in her deep sorrow is grayish-green like her Son. Amid life—its color, movement, and energy—death has us surrounded. Yet in His death, the Author of life has swallowed up death. Life's color, movement, and energy live eternally in Him.

161

Giovanni Benedetto Castiglione's painting depicts the cross and Christ Himself as low to the ground, in close proximity to the women gathered at His feet. The light emanating from our Savior demonstrates the power and radiance of His victory over death for His followers. The Church Father Venantius says, and the painting shows, "Darkness perishes, put to flight by the brightness of Christ; the thick pall of eternal night falls." In the presence of the cross, we can sing, "From the cross Thy wisdom shining Breaketh forth in conqu'ring might; From the cross forever beameth All Thy bright redeeming light."

Crucifixion itself was relatively bloodless, but the severe scourging Jesus underwent caused major blood loss and worsened His fluid depletion. Because He was too worn out to breathe, Jesus succumbed to exhaustion asphyxia. The energy necessary to raise His body to breathe would have exhausted Him. The inability to move air adequately in and out of the lungs, combined with insufficient energy to continue breathing, would have caused a state of terminal asphyxia or death by asphyxiation.

Other possibilities as causes of Jesus' death include dehydration, irregularity of the heart rhythm (cardiac arrhythmias), congestive heart failure, and the seeping and rupture of the areas around the heart and the heart itself (pericardial and cardiac effusions with cardiac tamponade and cardiac rupture).

Breaking the bones in the lower legs of the victim and piercing the thorax with a spear would have guaranteed death for an individual hanging on a cross, but the actual cause of death would most likely be the result of a multitude of factors. In the end, all of these physical traumas point toward the horrific nature of crucifixion and demonstrate the depth of the inhumanity we are capable of directing toward our fellow human beings.

Johann Sebastian Bach rejoices in the finality of the words "It is finished," because suffering and death are finished for Christ and for us.

It is accomplished! O comfort for the afflicted souls! The night of mourning now counts the final hour. The hero from Judah triumphs with power and closes the battle. It is accomplished! My precious Savior, let me ask you: since you by this time are nailed to the cross and have yourself said, "It is accomplished," have I been made free from death? Can I through your pain and death inherit the kingdom of heaven? Is redemption of all the world here? You can, in agony, it is true, say nothing; but you bow your head and exclaim in silence, "Yes." Jesus, you who were dead, but who now live without end, in the final throes of death, I turn myself nowhere, but to you, who made propitiation for me, O you dear Lord! Give me only what you have merited; more I do not desire!

In light of the intentionally slow and torturous nature of death by crucifixion, it has always been startling how quickly Jesus died. Even Pontius Pilate was surprised. The suddenness of Jesus' death suggests that some physically critical event occurred. One theory is that Jesus suffered a massive heart attack that destroyed the entire left ventricle and caused it to rupture. Another theory is that Jesus died of a cardiac arrhythmia or renal failure caused by the combination of blood loss and the severe loss of body fluids and electrolytes.

Regardless of the cause, the Synoptic Gospels indicate that Jesus cried out in a loud voice, then bowed His head and died. The Roman centurion and the guards, accustomed to the art of crucifixion, recognized the moment of Jesus' death.

In the end we can only postulate that Jesus' demise was the result of extreme exhaustion, dehydration, blood loss, hypovolemic shock, excruciating and unrelenting pain, interference of normal respirations, the buildup of carbon dioxide and lack of oxygen, with subsequent cardiac irregularities, failure, or heart attack.

What cannot be disputed is that Jesus indeed died *on the cross*. Because He suffered and died in the cruelest fashion imaginable as a result of our sin, Jesus has delivered us from the power of sin, the devil, and death.

Nicolas Tournier captures the moment Jesus bows His head and dies. The light that radiates from our Savior as He manifests the Father's glory in doing the Father's will illuminates the faces of Mary, John, Mary Magdalene, and one of the saints. We can pray with the psalmist, "In Your light do we see light" (Psalm 36:9).

The next time you view a crucifix (a cross with the body of Christ on it), reflect on what happened to Jesus on the cross. Consider His experiences in the Garden of Gethsemane. Relive His scourging at the hands of the Roman soldiers. Imagine the pain of being nailed to the cross. Envision what Jesus underwent as He pushed up on His feet, pulled up on His arms, and pushed His scourged back against the stipes in order to breathe. Remember that Jesus suffered and died for you and for the forgiveness of your sins. For that fact give God all thanks and praise.

The darkness of this painting by Pierre-Paul Prud'hon symbolizes the reality of Jesus' death and His confrontation with sin, death, and hell. Truly "He was cut off out of the land of the living" (Isaiah 53:8). Yet the darkness cannot consume the light. Although our Savior dies, yet shall He live. So we, groping in darkness and the shadow of death, will "see the light of life and be satisfied" (Isaiah 53:11 NIV).

The words of the Byzantine liturgy rehearse the death and burial of Jesus in this way:

Joseph went to Pilate, pleaded with him and cried out: Give me that Stranger Who since his youth has wandered as a Stranger. Give me that Stranger Upon whom I look with wonder, Seeing him a guest of death. Give me that Stranger whom envious men Estrange from the world. Give me that Stranger That I may bury him in a tomb, who being a stranger has no place Whereon to lay his head. . . . In such words did the honorable Joseph plead with Pilate. He took the Savior's body and, with fear, wrapped it in linen with spices. And he placed you in a tomb, O you who grant everlasting life and great mercy to us all.

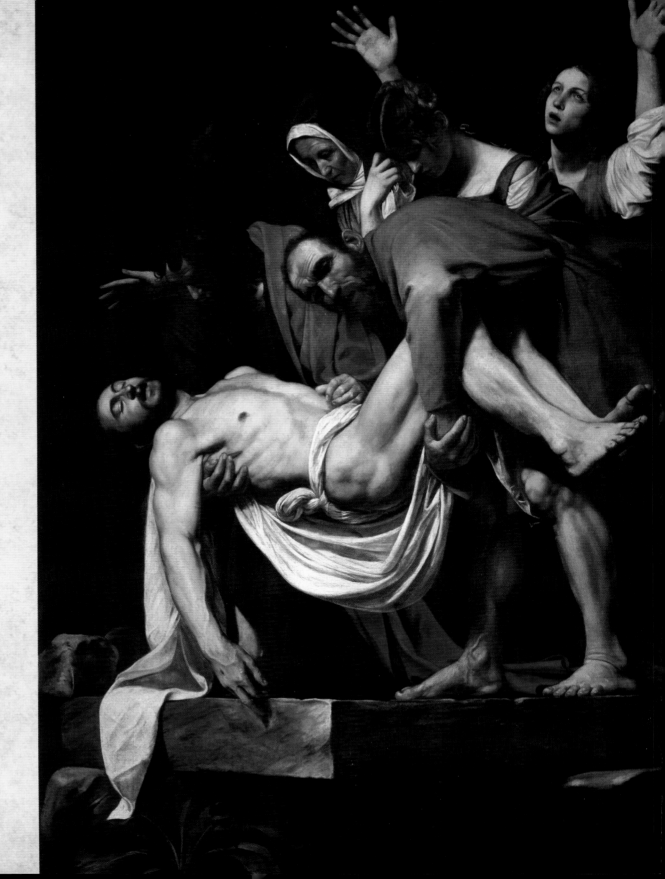

The believer shows faith in God's Son, Christ Jesus, by offering praise and thanks to God for the mercy and life that comes through Jesus' cross. This text from the Byzantine liturgy reflects such praise. The tree that the cross overcomes, which is referred to at the beginning, is the tree of the knowledge of good and evil in the Garden of Eden, the tree that occasioned the first sin.

By the tree of the cross you have healed the bitterness of the tree, and have opened Paradise to men. Glory be to you, Lord!

Now we are no longer prevented from coming to the tree of life; we have hope in your cross. Glory be to you, Lord!

O Immortal One, nailed to the wood, you have triumphed over the snares of the devil. Glory be to you, Lord!

You, who for my sake have submitted to being placed on the cross, accept my vigilant celebration of praise, O Christ, God, Friend of men.

Lord of the heavenly armies, who knows my carelessness of soul, save me by your cross, O Christ, God, Friend of men.

Brighter than fire, more luminous than flame, have you shown the wood of your cross, O Christ. Burn away the sins of the sick and enlighten the hearts of those who, with hymns, celebrate your voluntary crucifixion. Christ, God, glory to you!

Christ, God, who for us accepted a sorrowful crucifixion, accept all who sing hymns to your passion, and save us.

In Caravaggio's painting of the deposition of Jesus, our Savior's limp and lifeless body is, with much effort, lowered into the sarcophagus by Nicodemus (in the foreground) and John, the evangelist and disciple (at Jesus' head). Caravaggio invites us into the scene with the protruding corner of the sepulcher stone. Jesus' death is a reality for you in the present. Bent over and watching as He is laid to rest, Mary longs for her Son and His life. Next to her, Mary Magdalene, her hand on her head, reflects the disbelief and deep sorrow of all Jesus' followers. The final woman in the painting encompasses the entire scene with her hands raised in lamentation.

Reflecting on the events of the Passion of our Lord Jesus Christ shines light on the man Jesus as He gives Himself unconditionally to His Father. The Father's will is done. In reflecting on the crucifixion, we see Jesus suffer as a man and forgive as the Son of God.

Jesus' crucifixion shows love, understanding, and forgiveness in the face of sinners and sin. Christians trust in the mercy and forgiveness of God in Jesus Christ through His death and resurrection, and we continue the love, understanding, and forgiveness Jesus demonstrated on the cross in our lives of faith.

It is truly good, right, and salutary that we should at all times and in all places give thanks to You, holy Lord, almighty Father, everlasting God, through Jesus Christ, our Lord, who accomplished the salvation of mankind by the tree of the cross that, where death arose, there life also might rise again and that the serpent who overcame by the tree of the garden might likewise by the tree of the cross be overcome. Therefore with angels and archangels and with all the company of heaven we laud and magnify Your glorious name, evermore praising You.

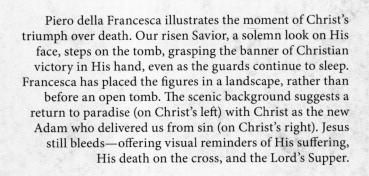

Piero della Francesca illustrates the moment of Christ's triumph over death. Our risen Savior, a solemn look on His face, steps on the tomb, grasping the banner of Christian victory in His hand, even as the guards continue to sleep. Francesca has placed the figures in a landscape, rather than before an open tomb. The scenic background suggests a return to paradise (on Christ's left) with Christ as the new Adam who delivered us from sin (on Christ's right). Jesus still bleeds—offering visual reminders of His suffering, His death on the cross, and the Lord's Supper.

The cross and resurrection are the life of faith of the Christian. In Baptism, we receive Christ in His death and resurrection and live as those put to death and resurrected in Him. Thus we can echo the words of Romanos:

Sing hymns to him, O earth-born; praise the one who suffered And died for you, and when in a short time You behold him living, receive him in your hearts; For Christ is going to be resurrected from the tomb and he will make you new. . . . Make ready for him a pure heart In order that your king will dwell in it, making a heaven. Only a short time now, and he will come to fill with joy those who are afflicted, In order that Adam might exult.

Chapter Five

THe Dead Shall Be Raised

The Resurrection of the Crucified One

Your cross I place before me;
Its saving pow'r restore me,
Sustain me in the test.
It will, when life is ending,
Be guiding and attending
My way to Your
eternal rest.

ΗΑΝΑΣΤΑΣΙΣ

Now on the first day of the week Mary Magdalene came to the tomb early, while it was still dark, and saw that the stone had been taken away from the tomb. So she ran and went to Simon Peter and the other disciple, the one whom Jesus loved, and said to them, "They have taken the Lord out of the tomb, and we do not know where they have laid Him." So Peter went out with the other disciple, and they were going toward the tomb. Both of them were running together, but the other disciple outran Peter and reached the tomb first. And stooping to look in, he saw the linen cloths lying there, but he did not go in. Then Simon Peter came, following him, and went into the tomb. He saw the linen cloths lying there, and the face cloth, which had been on Jesus' head, not lying with the linen cloths but folded up in a place by itself. Then the other disciple, who had reached the tomb first, also went in, and he saw and believed; for as yet they did not understand the Scripture, that He must rise from the dead. Then the disciples went back to their homes.

But Mary stood weeping outside the tomb, and as she wept she stooped to look into the tomb. And she saw two angels in white, sitting where the body of Jesus had lain, one at the head and one at the feet. They said to her, "Woman, why are you weeping?" She said to them, "They have taken away my Lord, and I do not know where they have laid Him." Having said this, she turned around and saw Jesus standing, but she did not know that it was Jesus. Jesus said to her, "Woman, why are you weeping? Whom are you seeking?" Supposing Him to be the gardener, she said to Him, "Sir, if you have carried Him away, tell me where you have laid Him, and I will take Him away." Jesus said to her, "Mary." She turned and said to Him in Aramaic, "Rabboni!" (which means Teacher). Jesus said to her, "Do not cling to Me, for I have not yet ascended to the Father; but go to My brothers and say to them, 'I am ascending to My Father and your Father, to My God and your God.'" Mary Magdalene went and announced to the disciples, "I have seen the Lord"—and that He had said these things to her.

John 20:1–18

The cross is again at the center of this icon, though Christ now holds it as His staff of victory. Clothed in the gold of kingship and the white of life, purity, and innocence, Christ emerges from His tomb to proclaim His victory and power over death, sin, sinners, and the devil! The *Arma Christi*—the nails, hammer, and ladder—lay broken in the tomb, devoid of power. The lock and key to Hades have been unlocked. The crucified Christ, the resurrection and the life, pulls the dead from the grave as Mary and the other believers look to "Jesus, the founder and perfecter of our faith, who for the joy that was set before Him endured the cross, despising the shame, and is seated at the right hand of the throne of God" (Hebrews 12:2).

Imagine if the journey through Lent and Holy Week ended with the service on Good Friday and there was no vigil to the celebration of Easter, no Easter Sunday service, no Easter joy. If that were the case, Paul's words to the Corinthian Christians would ring absolutely true, "If Christ has not been raised, your faith is futile and you are still in your sins. Then those also who have fallen asleep in Christ have perished. If in this life only we have hoped in Christ, we are of all people most to be pitied" (1 Corinthians 15:17–19). If the hope of Christians were only in Jesus' death, then pity would be the only thing appropriate for believers. If Jesus' death were the end of the story, then there is no hope for anyone.

But as Paul proclaims to the Christians in Rome, our Lord Jesus Christ "was delivered up for our trespasses and *raised for our justification*" (Romans 4:25).

The resurrection of the bodies of believers and life in the eternal kingdom of God is the end of the story of Christ Jesus and of those who believe in Him.

O God, creator of heaven and earth, grant that as the crucified body of Your dear Son was laid in the tomb and rested on this holy Sabbath, so we may await with Him the coming of the third day, and rise with Him to newness of life, who lives and reigns with You and the Holy Spirit, one God, now and forever. Amen.

There can be no doubt about the victory of Christ over sin, death, and hell in Albrecht Dürer's depiction of the resurrection. Christ's body, restored to life and vitality, stands atop His tomb. One hand makes the sign of blessing, peace, and mercy. The other hand bears the banner of victory. Christ is no longer subject to the cross, but the cross has been made subject to Him. And because of Christ's victory, death no longer can appall us.

Each chapter began with a stanza of Paul Gerhardt's Holy Week hymn "Upon the Cross Extended." It is only appropriate that our reflections on the Passion of Christ conclude with one of Gerhardt's Easter hymns, "Awake, My Heart, with Gladness."

Awake, my heart, with gladness,
See what today is done;
Now, after gloom and sadness,
Comes forth the glorious sun.
My Savior there was laid
Where our bed must be made
When to the realms of light
Our spirit wings its flight.

The foe in triumph shouted
When Christ lay in the tomb;
But lo, he now is routed,
His boast is turned to gloom.
For Christ again is free;
In glorious victory
He who is strong to save
Has triumphed o'er the grave.

This is a sight that gladdens—
What peace it doth impart!
Now nothing ever saddens
The joy within my heart.
No gloom shall ever shake,
No foe shall ever take
The hope which God's own Son
In love for me has won.

Now hell, its prince, the devil,
Of all their pow'r are shorn;
Now I am safe from evil,
And sin I laugh to scorn.
Grim death with all its might
Cannot my soul affright;
It is a pow'rless form,
Howe'er it rave and storm.

Now I will cling forever
To Christ, my Savior true;
My Lord will leave me never,
Whate'er He passes through.
He rends death's iron chain;
He breaks through sin and pain;
He shatters hell's grim thrall;
I follow Him through all.

He brings me to the portal
That leads to bliss untold,
Whereon this rhyme immortal
Is found in script of gold:
"Who there My cross has shared
Finds here a crown prepared;
Who there with Me has died
Shall here be glorified."

One reflects on the nature and details of Christ's suffering and death not to feel sorry for Him or to mourn Him or to make oneself feel even more guilty. One reflects on Jesus' Passion and cross to see God at work in Jesus and upon rebellious humanity. In hearing and experiencing that work of God, believers have life in Jesus' name (John 20:31).

These reflections on the Passion of Christ demonstrate that the suffering and death of Jesus was a real event. The Son of God suffered cruelly throughout His agony in the garden, His scourging and bearing of the cross, and His crucifixion. This cruel and inhuman way to die really happened to the Son of God.

And what really happened to Jesus occurred because of all humanity. As the reproaches in the Good Friday liturgy proclaim, "You have given Me over and delivered Me to those who persecute Me." The story of Christ's crucifixion and death is the story of the Son of God who came to have mercy on sinners, who was rejected and crucified by a humanity who will have nothing to do with a God who comes to have mercy on all. These reflections on the Passion of Christ should lead you to see your own hands stained by the whip, the hammer and nails, and the spear. Christ's Passion is your story of rebellion against God.

The Lamb of God was sacrificed at the hands of sinners but raised again to be the source of life for those who crucified Him. In this painting that is part of a massive altarpiece, Jan van Eyck presents Christ as the source of heavenly life and the center of heaven's praise.

The rebellion of humanity against God's Son is the very way God chooses to deal with sin, evil, suffering, and death—through the sin, suffering, and death of His Son. In the mystery of the cross, our rebellion is God's way of salvation, according to John L. McKenzie.

Jesus did not give us what we really ask: a rational explanation of the existence of suffering, and a demonstration how the terrible waste of human resources which suffering involves really contributes toward human fulfillment. He said that the Son of Man had to suffer; he did not say why. He accepted it and made it the medium of salvation; but he left it mysterious why this is the only means by which the saving act can be accomplished. His own death illustrates better than anything else his principle of not resisting evil. That evil is overcome by nonresistance has been comprehended by very few Christians. These few were convinced that Jesus presented in his words and life not only a good way of doing things, not only an ideal to be executed whenever it is convenient, but the only way of doing what he did.

This was the beginning of Jesus' victory. We confess in the Creed that He "descended into hell." He didn't go as others, as a helpless prisoner through a gate that would never open again. He descended into hell as the overlord of the dead. He broke through the gates. A revolution occurred on this day that changed the balance of power forever. The earthquakes that shook Jerusalem were a sign of this. The curtain in the temple that had blocked the way into the Holy of Holies, to God Himself, where no one dared to go except for the high priest on the Day of Atonement, was torn from top to bottom. Now it was opened so we sinners could go straight to God's fatherly arms. Even the gates of death were opened. Now, every knee, even those under the earth, will bow before Christ. Whoever believes in Christ need not fear death Christ goes before him.

—Bo Giertz

Yet just as Jesus' suffering and death is not the end of His story, so it is not the end of your story either. Jesus' suffering and death crucifies the rebellious person in you, and His resurrection raises you from the dead. It is an event that happens *to you*. As Paul says in his Epistle to the Romans, "For if we have been united with Him in a death like His, we shall certainly be united with Him in a resurrection like His" (6:5). It is, as Martin Luther says, the great exchange and reversal, Christ's life becomes ours and our life becomes His.

Here we have a most pleasing vision not only of communion but of a blessed struggle and victory and salvation and redemption. Christ is God and man in one person. He has neither sinned nor died, and is not condemned, and he cannot sin, die, or be condemned; his righteousness, life, and salvation are unconquerable, eternal, omnipotent. By the wedding ring of faith he shares in the sins, death, and pains of hell which are his bride's. As a matter of fact, he makes them his own and acts as if they were his own and as if he himself had sinned; he suffered, died, and descended into hell that he might overcome them all. Now since it was such a one who did all this, and death and hell could not swallow him up, these were necessarily swallowed up by him in a mighty duel; for his righteousness is greater than the sins of all men, his life stronger than death, his salvation more invincible than hell. Thus the believing soul by means of the pledge of its faith is free in Christ, its bridegroom, free from all sins, secure against death and hell, and is endowed with the eternal righteousness, life, and salvation of Christ its bridegroom.

In this painting by Lucas Cranach, Christ's victory over sin, death, and hell through His cross is central to the imagery. For example, to the left, the risen and victorious Christ stands atop death and slays the dragon—Satan. In the background are the Israelites, gazing upon the bronze serpent, an act which brought them salvation from the plague of snakes during their wilderness wandering. Cranach also includes the announcement of peace to the Bethlehem shepherds (center background). John the Baptist points to Christ, who is the fulfillment of all the messianic prophecies, while Martin Luther points to the Scriptures as the means to understand Jesus' crucifixion. The primary depiction of the reconciliation and victory that is ours through Christ is Cranach's inclusion of himself. Looking directly out of the painting, Cranach invites you to join him at the foot of the cross, where the blood of Christ pours over him, bringing cleansing from sin and reconciliation with God. Thus you can answer that you were there when they crucified the Lord because you continue to hear His Word preached, remember your Baptism, and receive the body and blood of the Crucified One in the Lord's Supper.

This traditional hymn for Good Friday announces what marks and precedes your living and your dying: the cross of your Savior, the banner that marks the end of the story.

The royal banners forward go;
The cross shows forth redemption's flow,
Where He, by whom our flesh was made,
Our ransom in His flesh has paid:

Where deep for us the spear was dyed,
Life's torrent rushing from His side,
To wash us in the precious flood!
Where flowed the water and the blood.

In his simple, serene painting of the crucifixion, Diego Rodriguez de Silva y Velasquez makes tangible the intensity of the pathos of Christ's suffering. Yet Velasquez's use of light to isolate the human form of Jesus' body against the deep black background brings to the forefront the glory of God in Jesus' human pathos. The suffering of God in Christ is the glory of the Suffering Servant Son of God. To know the Father is to see Him through this light: the willing suffering of His Son. In this seeing is fulfilled the psalmist's words: "For with You is the fountain of life; in Your light do we see light" (Psalm 36:9). In this seeing, this faith, "is the victory that has overcome the world" (1 John 5:4).

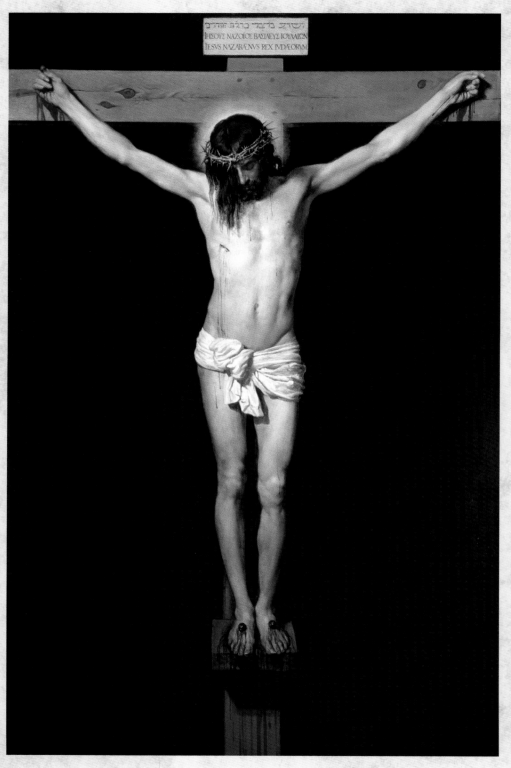

What happens to Christ happens to you, and the end of the story for Him is the end of the story for you. This is where reflection on the Passion of Christ leads. The dead shall be raised. The One who suffered and was crucified has been raised from the dead. Your Baptism into Jesus' suffering, death, and resurrection will be completed on the Last Day when you, who were crucified in Him, will be raised. "In a moment, in the twinkling of an eye, at the last trumpet . . . the dead will be raised" (1 Corinthians 15:52). That truly is the end of the story.

This traditional hymn for Good Friday trumpets the ending of the fray for you.

Sing, my tongue, the glorious battle;
Sing the ending of the fray.
Now above the cross, the trophy,
Sound the loud triumphant lay;
Tell how Christ, the world's redeemer,
As a victim won the day.

Thus, with thirty years accomplished,
He went forth from Nazareth,
Destined, dedicated, willing,
Did His work, and met His death;
Like a lamb He humbly yielded
On the cross His dying breath.

Faithful cross, true sign of triumph,
Be for all the noblest tree;
None in foliage, none in blossom,
None in fruit thine equal be;
Symbol of the world's redemption,
For the weight that hung on thee!

The cross is the symbol of the world's redemption. It is the symbol of your redemption. Look at the cross! In it you see death's end and life's beginning for you. Here the Crucified and Resurrected One is welcoming you with open arms from His cross of mercy to Himself. His death is your death, and His resurrection is your life.

This prayer proclaims Christ's death as the end of your death and His life as the beginning of your eternal life.

It is truly good, right, and salutary that we should at all times and in all places give thanks to You, holy Lord, almighty Father, everlasting God. And most especially are we bound to praise You on this day for the glorious resurrection of Your Son, Jesus Christ, the very Paschal Lamb, who was sacrificed for us and bore the sins of the world. By His dying He has destroyed death, and by His rising again He has restored to us everlasting life. Therefore with Mary Magdalene, Peter and John, and with all the witnesses of the resurrection, with angels and archangels, and with all the company of heaven we laud and magnify Your glorious name, evermore praising You.

Let no one grieve at his poverty,
for the universal kingdom has been revealed.
Let no one mourn that he has fallen again and again;
for forgiveness has risen from the grave.
Let no one fear death,
for the death of our Savior has set us free.
He has destroyed it by enduring it.

He destroyed hell when He descended into it.
He put it into an uproar even as it tasted of His flesh.
Isaiah foretold this when he said,
"You, O hell, have been troubled by
encountering Him below."

Hell was in an uproar because it was done away with.
It was in an uproar because it is mocked.
It was in an uproar, for it is destroyed.
It is in an uproar, for it is annihilated.
It is in an uproar, for it is now made captive.
Hell took a body, and discovered God.
It took earth, and encountered heaven.
It took what it saw,
and was overcome by what it did not see.

O death, where is thy sting?
O hell, where is thy victory?

Christ is risen, and you, O death, are annihilated!
Christ is risen, and the evil ones are cast down!
Christ is risen, and the angels rejoice!
Christ is risen, and life is liberated!
Christ is risen, and the tomb is emptied of its dead;
for Christ having risen from the dead,
is become the firstfruits of those who have fallen asleep.
To Him be glory and power forever and ever. Amen!

—John Chrysostom

Any reflection on the Passion of Jesus must lead from the cross to the empty tomb and the living witness of those who saw Jesus risen from the dead, alive in the flesh. Lent and Good Friday must end in Easter!

That is where these reflections on the significance of the Lord's Passion also end. These reflections were meant to lead to one thing: life by faith for you in the Crucified and Resurrected One.

Mathias Gruenewald's painting for the altar in Isenheim, Germany, does not end at Good Friday. Rather, it rejoices in Christ's Easter victory. The Crucified One is the risen, glorified, and life-giving One. Christ is the Light, the Resurrection, and the Life of all people. A halo of light suffuses Jesus, recalling the rainbow of life following the flood and the brightness of Christ at His transfiguration. Jesus seems powerfully propelled out of the tomb, as if death could not hold Him. The grave is broken. Thrust to the ground by the power of the resurrection explosion, the soldiers are cast aside. Evil is over-turned. Peace reigns as evidenced by the marks of the crucifixion, prominently shining toward us as the Son of God raises His hands in blessing.

Appendix

The Shroud of Turin

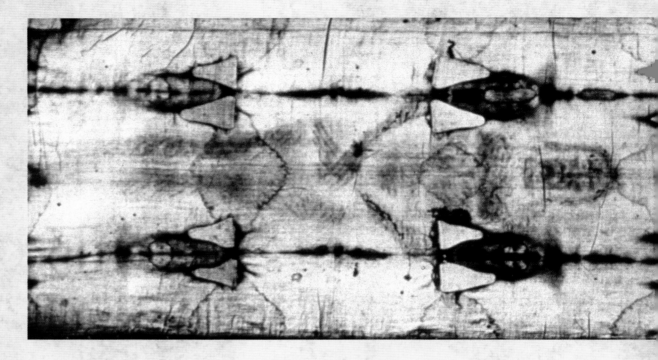

From the Gospel accounts of the burial of Jesus Christ, it appears that He was buried in haste because of the Jewish Sabbath. The evangelist Mark specifically points out that the burial of Jesus was performed in haste. All of the biblical accounts mention that Jesus was wrapped in a linen shroud or wrappings of cloth or fine linen. This burial cloth or shroud would have been used in the typical Jewish manner to envelop the body in its entirety, wrapping it lengthwise. John provides further detail when he notes that Jesus' body, in accordance with Jewish burial customs, was bound up in wrappings of cloth along with perfumed oils. Yet the complete anointing with oils and Jewish entombment process was apparently postponed for the following day.

Many people believe that the famous Shroud of Turin is the burial cloth that enveloped Jesus after His crucifixion as He was laid in His tomb. The Shroud of Turin derives its name from Turin, Italy, where it is kept in the Cathedral of St. John the Baptist.

Tracing the historical existence of the shroud prior to its first-known exposition in Lirey, France, in 1357 has proven difficult indeed. After its exposition in Lirey, it was moved to Chambery, France, where it was involved in a church fire in 1532. It was apparently folded and stored in a metal container that partially melted during this fire. Many of the more obvious markings on the shroud are scorch marks sustained in that fire, for example, two long parallel lines running the entire length of the cloth. Some burn marks were patched with diamond-shaped pieces of cloth. The triangular shaped marks in the cloth were caused by the melting storage box dripping onto the folded cloth during the fire. In addition to the burn marks are the blood stains one might expect to find on the cloth used to wrap a body that had died after sustaining trauma.

Worldwide interest in the cloth began in 1898 when Secondo Pia took photos of the shroud during an exposition at the church in Turin, Italy. His negatives revealed the image of a man who had apparently been crucified. The amazing fact was that his photographic image was a positive image of the negative photographic plate. This meant that he must have photographed what was actually a negative image. It must be remembered that photographers usually work with negative images of positive photographic images, not the other way around. This simple fact has stimulated controversy that exists even to this day regarding how this unique phenomenon occurred. What was discovered on the photographic images from 1898 has led to extensive study through the years. As a result, the Shroud of Turin probably has become the most studied religious artifact in history.

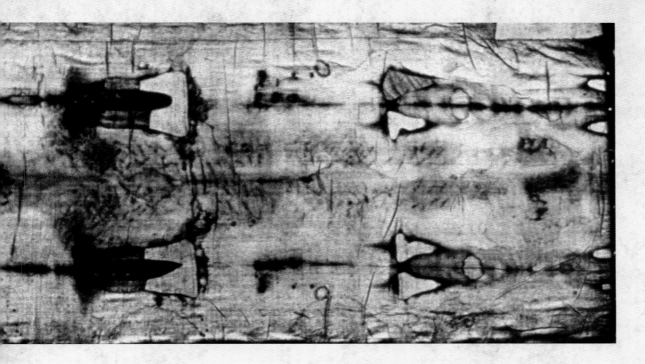

The shroud itself is a long piece of linen cloth measuring fourteen feet in length and three feet in width. The cloth is imprinted with the image of a man who appears to have been crucified. The man's head appears to have been beaten severely in the face and had a crown or cap of thorns placed on it. In addition, the man's shoulders would seem to indicate he had carried something heavy across the top of his shoulders. The image also reveals the man underwent a severe whipping.

Such a burial cloth would have been wrapped under the backside of the individual, starting at the feet and proceeding toward and over the head. The shroud would then have continued down the front of the body, wrapping once again under the feet. When the entire Shroud of Turin is unfolded, it shows such a pattern with the image of what is believed to be the body of Jesus Christ.

The image on the shroud is of a man with long hair, full moustache, long beard, and closed eyes. He has swollen cheekbones, and the bridge of his nose also appears swollen. There are bloodstains on the forehead, and the back of the head is covered with what appears to be bloodstains from puncture wounds. There are many marks across the victim's back, actually more than one hundred, in groups of two's or three's. These appear to cover the entire body. The shroud shows darkened quadrangular areas on each shoulder and the upper back that could have been caused by carrying a heavy object placed across the shoulders. The object in question would have weighed approximately one hundred pounds. Bloodstains from the

Because for our sake you tasted gall, may the enemy's bitterness be killed in us. Because for our sake you drank sour wine, may what is weak in us be strengthened. Because for our sake you were spat upon, may we be bathed in the dew of immortality. Because for our sake you were struck with a rod, may we receive shelter in the last. Because for our sake you accepted a crown of thorns, may we who love you be crowned with garlands that never can fade. Because for our sake you were wrapped in a shroud, may we be clothed in your all-enfolding strength. Because you were laid in the new grave and the tomb, may we receive renewal of soul and body. Because you rose and returned to life, may we be brought to life again.

—*Fifth-century Communion hymn*

wrists flow in two different angles, both sixty-five degrees and fifty-five degrees from horizontal. Questions about how the blood could have run in the first place, especially at two different angles, have spurred tremendous controversy about how the nails were placed through the wrists or hands. This also has created discussion about how the victim could have moved on the cross. The image on the shroud shows that the right foot of the victim was nailed onto the cross first, then the left foot was nailed over the top of the right.

One of the most significant controversies surrounding the Shroud of Turin deals with how the image was produced on the cloth. Attempts have been made to reproduce the shroud's image in order to prove that it could not be the shroud used at the burial of Jesus. Yet no one has been able to reproduce an image that contains all of the Shroud of Turin's particular characteristics. Countless attempts have tried to reproduce the phenomena of the shroud by means of painting, photography, staining, and so on. All have been easily discredited.

With regard to how the image may have been generated on the shroud, the most likely theory, but one that cannot be reproduced, is lactic acid staining. This theory proposes that the victim sustained severe renal damage from kidney trauma caused during the scourging. Coupled with the dehydration that would have occurred during the entire crucifixion process, the renal damage caused a buildup of lactic acid in the body. The lactic acid would have been excreted through the extreme perspiration suffered during the crucifixion. The lactic acid from the perspiration would have oxidized the cellulose in the cloth, and the image would have formed over a period of time. Although this theory is attractive, the exact nature of how the image came to appear on the shroud has never been proven.

Years of intense research on the Shroud of Turin have yielded tremendous insight into the horror of crucifixion. Analysis of the image vividly portrays the destruction of skin over the entire body caused by the scourging. The method of affixing the hands and feet to the cross is clearly shown, as is the terrible facial beating the victim underwent. Amazingly, the image on the shroud also shows a spear wound in the right chest wall, just as was described by the disciples in order to prove that Jesus actually died.

In all its mystery and with all the study and investigation it has generated, the Shroud of Turin seems to have created more controversy and more questions than it has ever answered. Regardless of whether it is the shroud of Jesus, it is the one piece of archaeological evidence that helps us study scourging and crucifixion. For this purpose, it has been invaluable. Whether one believes the Shroud of Turin is the burial cloth of the Lord Jesus Christ, it still depicts a victim who had been beaten in the face, scourged across his entire body, crowned with a cap of thorns, forced to carry a heavy weight, and nailed to a cross. This is certainly the image of a man who suffered a violent and terrible death.

For Further Reading

Barbet, Pierre, MD. *A Doctor at Calvary*. Translated by the Earl of Wicklow. New York: P. J. Kenedy, 1953.

Bishop, Jim. *The Day Christ Died*. New York, Harper, 1957.

Edwards, William, MD. "On the Physical Death of Jesus Christ." *Journal of the American Medical Association* 255:11 (March 21, 1986): 1455–63.

Hengel, Martin. *Crucifixion in the Ancient World and the Folly of the Message of the Cross*. Philadelphia: Fortress, 1989.

Holoubek, J., MD. "Execution by Crucifixion: History, Methods and Cause of Death." *Journal of Medicine* 26:1–2 (1995): 1–16.

McDowell, Josh. *The Resurrection Factor*. Nashville: Nelson, 1993.

Neuhaus, Richard John. *Death on a Friday Afternoon*. New York: Basic Books, 2000.

Schwortz, Barrie, ed. www.shroud.com (Shroud of Turin Web site).

Stevenson, Kenneth, and Gary Habermas. *Verdict on the Shroud*. Wayne, PA: Dell/Banbury Books, 1981.

Acknowledgments

I must again thank Father Harry McAlpine for his encouragement to pursue putting my words on paper.

I would like to acknowledge Dr. William Edwards of the Mayo Clinic, whose inspiring article "On the Physical Death of Jesus Christ" has been the cornerstone for my lectures and this book. Thanks also go to three authors whose works have contributed much to my understanding and appreciation of Christ's Passion: Martin Hengel, Dr. Pierre Barbet, and Josh McDowell.

Writing this book has given me a new appreciation for the Gospel accounts of Matthew, Mark, Luke, and John, who under the inspiration of the Holy Spirit documented the life and teachings of Jesus of Nazareth.

To my family, friends, and above-mentioned authors, let me simply say thank you!

—Gerard Joseph Stanley Sr., MD

Half Title
Artwork: Detail of Diego Rodriguez de Silva y Velasquez (1599–1660), *Christ on the Cross*, ca. 1630 (oil on canvas). © Prado, Madrid, Spain/The Bridgeman Art Library.

Page 6
Artwork: Peter Paul Rubens, *The Entombment*, ca. 1612 (oil on canvas). Photo courtesy of J. Paul Getty Museum, Los Angeles, California.

Page 8
Artwork: Rogier (Roger) van der Weyden (ca. 1399–1464), detail of *The Crucifixion, with the Virgin and Saint John the Evangelist Mourning*, ca. 1450–55 (oil and gold on panel). John G. Johnson Collection, Philadelphia Museum of Art, Philadelphia, Pennsylvania. Photo: The Philadelphia Museum of Art/Art Resource, NY.

Page 9
Prayer: Litany of the Passion, trans. by Alcuin L. Mikulanis, OFM, from *Come, Lord Jesus*. Copyright © 1976, 1981, Lucien Deiss. Published by World Library Publications, Franklin Park, IL. www.wlpmusic.com, 800-566-6150. All rights reserved. Used by permission.

Page 10
Artwork: Hans Memling (ca. 1433–94), *The Passion*, 1470–71 (oil on panel). © Galleria Sabauda, Turin, Italy/Alinari/The Bridgeman Art Library.

Page 11
Prayer: From *Ancestral Prayers*, © 1976. Reprinted with permission of Templegate Publishers, Springfield, Illinois, www.templegate.com

Hymn: "Upon the Cross Extended," public domain.

The author references the article by William D. Edwards, Wesley J. Gabel, and Floyd E. Hosmer, "On the Physical Death of Jesus Christ," *Journal of the American Medical Association* 255, no. 11 (March 21, 1986): 1455–63.

Page 13
Artwork: William C. Severson, *St. Luke the Physician*. Photo courtesy of the Rev. Prof. Robert V. Roethemeyer and Concordia Theological Seminary, Fort Wayne, Indiana.

Page 14
Artwork: Albrecht Dürer, from *Small Passion*.

Hymn: "Upon the Cross Extended," public domain.

Page 15
Artwork: Albrecht Dürer, from *Small Passion*.

Page 16
Artwork: Albrecht Dürer, from *Small Passion*.

Page 17
Artwork: Albrecht Dürer, from *Small Passion*.

Quotation from Martin Luther: Eugene F. A. Klug, ed., *The Complete Sermons of Martin Luther*, vol. 5, trans. Eugene F. A. Klug et al. Copyright © 2000 Baker Books, a division of Baker Publishing Group.

Page 18
Artwork: Antonio Ciseri (1821–91), *Ecco Homo* (oil on canvas). © Galleria d'Arte Moderna, Florence, Italy/The Bridgeman Art Library.

Page 19
Hymn: Meropius Pontius Paulinus, *Carmina* 19, 718–30 (*Patrologia Latina* 61:550). From Costante Berselli, ed., *Hymns to Christ*, trans. Sister Mary of Jesus (Middlegreen, England: St. Paul Publications, 1982). Used wih permission.

Page 20
Prayer: Collect for Monday of Holy Week, *Lutheran Service Book: Altar Book*, © 2006 Concordia Publishing House.

Hymn: "Upon the Cross Extended," public domain.

Page 21
Artwork: Ferdinando Gallego, *Jesus Christ Blessing* (central panel of a retable). Museo del Prado, Madrid, Spain. Photo: Erich Lessing/Art Resource, NY.

Page 22
Artwork: Jacob Jordaens (1593–1678), *The Four Evangelists* (oil on wood). Louvre, Paris, France. Photo: Réunion des Musées Nationaux/Art Resource, NY.

Page 23
Quotations "Drawing on this rich treasure" and "the theology of the evangelists": From Reginald C. Fuller, gen. ed., *A New Catholic Commentary on Holy Scripture* (Nashville: Thomas Nelson, 1969), 807, 808.

Page 25
Artwork: Benjamin Robert Haydon, *Christ's Entry into Jerusalem*. Mount St. Mary's Seminary, Cincinnati, Ohio. Image courtesy of The Athenaeum of Ohio. Photo © Don Denney.

Quotation "The apostles, companions of Jesus": From Reginald C. Fuller, gen. ed., *A New Catholic Commentary on Holy Scripture* (Nashville: Thomas Nelson, 1969), 807.

Page 26
Artwork: Rembrandt Harmenszoon van Rijn (1606–69), *The Three Crosses*, 1653 (etching). © British Museum, London, United Kingdom/The Bridgeman Art Library.

Page 29
Artwork: Francisco de Zurbaran (1598–1664), *Crucified Christ*. Museao de Bellas Artes, Seville, Spain. Photo: Alinari/Art Resource, NY.

Page 30
Artwork: Jacopo Robusti Tintoretto (1518–94), *The Crucifixion of Christ*, 1565.

© Scuola Grande di San Rocco, Venice, Italy/The Bridgeman Art Library.

Page 33

Artwork: Lucas Cranach the Elder (1472–1553), *The Crucifixion*, 1503 (oil on panel). © Alte Pinakothek, Munich, Germany/Giraudon/The Bridgeman Art Library.

Page 34

Artwork: *Crucifixion* icon (tempera on panel) by Byzantine (fourteenth century). © Byzantine Museum, Athens, Greece/The Bridgeman Art Library.

Quotation: Adrian Nocent, *The Liturgical Year*, vol. 3 (Collegeville, MN: Liturgical Press, 1977). Copyright 1977 by The Order of St. Benedict, Inc. Published by Liturgical Press, Collegeville, Minnesota. Reprinted with permission.

Page 36

Prayer: Proper Preface, Common I, *Lutheran Service Book: Altar Book*, © 2006 Concordia Publishing House.

Page 37

Artwork: Salvador Dalí, *Christ of Saint John of the Cross*. Glasgow Museums, The St. Mungo Museum of Religious Life and Art. Photo courtesy of Artothek.

Hymn: "Hail, Thou Once Despised Jesus," public domain.

Page 38

Artwork: Caravaggio (Michelangelo Merisi), *The Taking of Christ*. Courtesy of the National Gallery of Ireland and the Jesuit Community, Leeson St., Dublin, who acknowledge the generosity of the late Dr. Marie-Lea Wilson. Photo © The National Gallery of Ireland.

Page 39

Hymn: "Upon the Cross Extended," public domain.

Prayer: Collect for Holy Tuesday, *Lutheran Service Book: Altar Book*, © 2006 Concordia Publishing House.

Page 40

The Sanctus combines Isaiah 6:3 and Matthew 21:9. In most orders of worship, the Sanctus is part of the liturgy of the Service of the Sacrament.

Page 41

Artwork: Pietro Lorenzetti (ca. 1284–after 1345), *Entry of Christ into Jerusalem* (fresco). © Church of St. Francis, Assisi, Umbria, Italy/Alinari/The Bridgeman Art Library.

Page 42

Artwork: Detail of the entry into Jerusalem from the sarcophagus of Junius Bassus. Museum of the Treasury, St. Peter's Basilica, Vatican State. Photo: Scala/Art Resource, NY.

Page 44

Quotation from Jerome: *Commentary on Matthew* 4.26.41. Taken from *Matthew 14–28* (ACCS) edited by Manlio Simonetti. Copyright © 2002 by the Institute of Classical Christian Studies (ICCS), Thomas C. Oden & Manlio Simonetti. Use by permission of InterVarsity Press, PO Box 1400, Downers Grove, IL 60515. ivpress.com

Page 45

Artwork: Sebastiano Ricci (1659–1734), *Christ on the Mount of Olives*, 1730. Kunsthistorisches Museum, Vienna, Austria. Photo: Erich Lessing/Art Resource, NY.

Page 46

Artwork: Sandro Botticelli (1444/5–1510), *The Agony in the Garden*, ca. 1500 (oil on canvas). © Capilla Real, Granada, Spain/Giraudon/The Bridgeman Art Library.

Quotation from Martin Luther: Ewald M. Plass, comp., *What Luther Says*, pp. 1349–50, copyright © 1959 Concordia Publishing House.

Page 47

Artwork: Giovanni Guercino, *Christ in Gethsemane*, 1620. Photo courtesy of Superstock.

Quotation from Ephrem the Syrian: *Commentary on Tatian's* Diatessaron. From C. McCarthy, trans., *St. Ephrem's Commentary on Tatian's* Diatessaron (Oxford: Oxford University Press, 1993), 292–96. By permission of Oxford University Press, Inc.

Page 48

Artwork: Giovanni Canavesio (1450–1500), detail of *Christ in the Garden of Olives*, 1492 (fresco). Chapelle Notre Dame des Fontaines, La Brigue, Alpes Maritimes, France.

Page 49

Quotation from Martin Luther: Eugene F. A. Klug, ed., *The Complete Sermons of Martin Luther*, vol. 5, trans. Eugene F. A. Klug et al. Copyright © 2000 Baker Books, a division of Baker Publishing Group.

Page 50

Quotation from Martin Luther: Ewald M. Plass, comp., *What Luther Says*, p. 1423, © 1959 Concordia Publishing House.

Page 51

Artwork: Jan Gossaert (Mabuse) (ca. 1478–1532), *Agony in the Garden*, ca. 1509–10 (oil on oak). Gemaeldegalerie, Staatliche Museen zu Berlin, Berlin, Germany. Photo: Bildarchiv Preussischer Kulturbesitz/Art Resource, NY.

Page 52

Artwork: Benvenuto di Giovanni, *The Agony in the Garden*, ca. 1491 (tempera on panel). Samuel H. Kress Collection. Image courtesy of the Board of Trustees, National Gallery of Art, Washington DC.

Page 53

Quotation: Tertullian, *On Flight Amid Persecution* 8.

Page 54

Quotation: Augustine, *Sermon* 302.3. From *The Works of Saint Augustine: A Translation for the 21st Century*. Edited by J. E. Rotelle. New York: New City Press, 1990–. Used with permission.

Page 55

Artwork: Master of Saint Francis (thirteenth century), *Crucifixion*, from Umbria (wood, painted cross). Louvre, Paris, France. Photo: Erich Lessing/Art Resource, NY.

Page 56

Artwork: Albrecht Dürer, from *Engraved Passion*.

Page 57

Quotation from Ignatius of Antioch: *Letter to the Romans* (Patrologia Graeca 5:692). From Costante Berselli, ed., *Hymns to Christ*, trans. Sister Mary of Jesus (Middlegreen, England: St. Paul Publications, 1982), 12. Used with permission.

Page 58

Quotation from Martin Luther: Eugene F. A. Klug, ed., *The Complete Sermons of Martin Luther*, vol. 5, trans. Eugene F. A. Klug et al. Copyright © 2000 Baker Books, a division of Baker Publishing Group.

Page 59

Artwork: Lucas Cranach the Elder (completed by Lucas Cranach the Younger), Altar der Peter und Paulkirche in Weimar, Germany. Mitteltafel: Christus am Freuz. Weimar, Stadtpfarrkirche. Photo by Constantin Beyer, Artothek.

Page 60

Artwork: David Alfaro Siqueiros (1896–1974), *Christ*. Collezione d'Arte Religiosa Moderna, Vatican Museums, Vatican State. © 2008 Artists Rights Society (ARS), New York/SOMAAP, Mexico City. Photo: Scala/Art Resource, NY.

Page 61

Prayer: Proper Preface, Common II, *Lutheran Service Book: Altar Book*, © 2006 Concordia Publishing House.

Page 62
Artwork: Guercino (Giovanni Francesco Barbieri) (1591–1666), *The Betrayal of Christ*, ca. 1621 (oil on canvas). © Fitzwilliam Museum, University of Cambridge, United Kingdom/The Bridgeman Art Library.

Page 63
Hymn: "Upon the Cross Extended," public domain.
Prayer: Collect for Wednesday of Holy Week, *Lutheran Service Book: Altar Book*, © 2006 Concordia Publishing House.

Page 64
Artwork: Albrecht Dürer, from *Small Passion*.
Hymn: "Tomorrow Is My Dancing Day," public domain.

Page 65
Artwork: Albrecht Dürer, from *Small Passion*.
Hymn: "Christ, the Life of All the Living," public domain.

Page 66
Artwork: Caravaggio (Michelangelo Merisi da) (1573–1610), *Ecce Homo*. Palazzo Rosso, Genoa, Italy. Photo: Scala/Art Resource, NY.

Page 67
Quotation from Martin Luther: Eugene F. A. Klug, ed., *The Complete Sermons of Martin Luther*, vol. 5, trans. Eugene F. A. Klug et al. Copyright © 2000 Baker Books, a division of Baker Publishing Group.

Page 68
Quotation: From *The Lenten Triodion* translated from the original Greek by Mother Mary and Archimandrite Kallistos Ware (London: Faber & Faber, 1978).

Page 69
Artwork: Albrecht Dürer, from *Small Passion*.
Quotation: Cyril of Alexandria, *Commentary on the Gospel of John*.

Page 70
Artwork: Hieronymus Bosch (1450–1516), *Christ Mocked (The Crowning with Thorns)*, ca. 1490–1500 (oil on panel). © National Gallery, London, United Kingdom/The Bridgeman Art Library.
Quotation: Michael Marissen, *Lutheranism, Anti-Judaism, and Bach's* St. John Passion (New York: Oxford University Press, 1998), 54. By permission of Oxford University Press, Inc.

Page 71
Artwork: Detail of Claude Mellan, *The Sudarium of Saint Veronica*, 1649 (engraving). Rosenwald Collection. Image courtesy of the Board of Trustees, National Gallery of Art, Washington DC.
Quotation: Clement of Alexandria, *Christ the Educator* 2.8.

Page 72
Artwork: Albrecht Dürer, from the *Engraved Passion*.
Poem: Hallgrimur Petursson, *Thirty-one Meditations on Christ's Passion*, trans. Charles V. Pilcher (Bynam, TX: Repristination Press, 2003), 21–22.

Page 74
Artwork: Lorenzo Monaco, *Pieta*, 1404 (tempera on wood). Uffizi, Florence, Italy. Photo: Erich Lessing/Art Resource, NY.

Page 75
Artwork: Diego Rodriguez de Silva y Velasquez (1599–1660), *Christ after the Flagellation Contemplated by the Christian Soul*, ca. 1628–29 (oil on canvas). © National Gallery, London, United Kingdom/The Bridgeman Art Library.
Prayer: R. A. Lipsius and M. Bonnet, eds., *Acta Apostolorum Apocrypha* (n.p., 1891–1903), 2:268. From Costante Berselli, ed., *Hymns to Christ*, trans. Sister Mary of Jesus (Middlegreen, England: St. Paul Publications, 1982), 34. Used with permission.

Pages 76–77
Artwork: *Arma Christi* images from German devotional booklet. © V&A Images, Victoria and Albert Museum, London, United Kingdom.

Page 77
Quotation: Tertullian, *The Chaplet* 13. Taken from *John 11–21* (ACCS) edited by Joel C. Elowsky. Copyright © 2007 by the Institute of Classical Christian Studies (ICCS), Thomas C. Oden & Joel C. Elowsky. Used with permission of InterVarsity Press, PO Box 1400, Downers Grove, IL 60515. ivpress.com

Page 78
Quotation: Michael Marissen, *Lutheranism, Anti-Judaism, and Bach's* St. John Passion (New York: Oxford University Press, 1998), 55. By permission of Oxford University Press, Inc.

Page 79
Artwork: Albrecht Dürer, from *Engraved Passion*.
Quotation: Romanus Melodus, *Kontakion on the Passion of Christ* 20.13–14. Reprinted from page 212 of *Kontakia of Romanos, Byzantine Melodist I: On the Person of Christ* translated and annotated by Marjorie Carpenter, by permission of the University of Missouri Press. Copyright © 1970 by the Curators of the University of Missouri.

Page 80
Artwork: Caravaggio (Michelangelo Merisi da) (1573–1610), *Christ at the Column*, 1606–7 (oil on canvas). Musee des Beaux-Arts, Rouen, France. Photo: Réunion des Musées Nationaux/Art Resource, NY.
Quotation: Cyril of Alexandria, *Commentary on the Gospel of John*.

Page 83
Artwork: Quentin Massys (or Metsys) (ca. 1466–1530), *Ecce Homo* (oil on canvas). © Palazzo Ducale, Venice, Italy/Cameraphoto Arte Venezia/The Bridgeman Art Library.

Page 84
Artwork: Jan Mostaert, *Christ Crowned with Thorns*. © The National Gallery, London, United Kingdom.

Page 85
Quotation from Dr. Edwards: William D. Edwards, Wesley J. Gabel, and Floyd E. Hosmer, "On the Physical Death of Jesus Christ," *Journal of the American Medical Association* 255, no. 11 (March 21, 1986): 1458.

Page 87
Artwork; Benvenuto di Giovanni, *Christ Carrying the Cross*, ca. 1491 (tempera on panel). Samuel H. Kress Collection. Image courtesy of the Board of Trustees, National Gallery of Art, Washington DC.

Page 88
Artwork: Jacopo Bassano, *The Way to Calvary*. © The National Gallery, London, United Kingdom.

Page 89
Quotation: Romanus Melodus, *Kontakion on Abraham and Isaac* 41.22–23. Reprinted from page 69 of *Kontakia of Romanos, Byzantine Melodist II: On Christian Life* translated and annotated by Marjorie Carpenter, by permission of the University of Missouri Press. Copyright © 1973 by the Curators of the University of Missouri.

Page 90
Artwork: Domenichino (Domenico Zampieri), *The Way to Calvary*, ca. 1610 (oil on copper). Photo courtesy of J. Paul Getty Museum, Los Angeles, California.

Page 91
Quotation: Cyril of Alexandria, *Commentary on the Gospel of John*.
Hymn text in caption: From "My Song Is Love Unknown," public domain.

Page 92
Quotation: Reprinted with the permission of Scribner, a Division of Simon Schuster, Inc., from pp. 90–91 of

The Cost of Discipleship by Dietrich Bonhoeffer. Copyright © 1959 by SCM Press Ltd. All rights reserved.

Page 93
Artwork: Albrecht Dürer, from *Large Passion*.
Quotation: Chromatius, *Tractate on Matthew 19.5*. Taken from *Matthew 14–28* (ACCS) edited by Manlio Simonetti. Copyright © 2002 by the Institute of Classical Christian Studies (ICCS), Thomas C. Oden & Manlio Simonetti. Used with permission of InterVarsity Press, PO Box 1400, Downers Grove, IL 60515. ivpress.com

Page 94
Artwork: Francesco di Giorgio Martini (1439–1502), *Despoiling of Christ*. Pinacoteca Nazionale, Siena, Italy. Photo: Scala/Art Resource, NY.

Page 95
Quotation: Michael Marissen, *Lutheranism, Anti-Judaism, and Bach's St. John Passion* (New York: Oxford University Press, 1998), 60. By permission of Oxford University Press, Inc.

Page 97
Artwork: Giandomenico Tiepolo (1727–1804), *The Way of the Cross, Station 10, Christ Is Stripped of His Garments* (oil on canvas). S. Polo, Venice, Italy. Photo: Cameraphoto Arte, Venice/Art Resource, NY.
Prayer: Proper Preface, Common III, *Lutheran Service Book: Altar Book*, © 2006 Concordia Publishing House.

Page 98
Artwork: Peter Paul Rubens (1577–1640), *Christ on the Cross*, ca. 1612 (oil on oak). Alte Pinakothek, Munich, Germany. Photo: Scala/Art Resource, NY.

Page 99
Hymn: "Upon the Cross Extended," public domain.
Prayer: Collect for Holy (Maundy) Thursday, *Lutheran Service Book: Altar Book*, © 2006 Concordia Publishing House.

Page 100
Quotation from Origen: From *A Word in Season* © 1981. Reprinted with permission of the Friends of Henry Ashworth, Augustinian Press. All rights reserved.

Page 101
Artwork: *The Crucifixion of Christ*, plaque from an ivory casket, Late Roman, ca. AD 425. British Museum, London, United Kingdom. © British Museum/Art Resource, NY.

Page 102
Artwork: Antonello da Messina (1430–79), *Calvary* or *Christ Between Two Thieves with Mary and St. John*, 1475 (oil on panel). © Koninklijk Museum voor Schone Kunsten, Antwerp, Belgium/Giraudon/The Bridgeman Art Library.
Prayer: From *Praise God: Common Prayer at Taizé*, edited and translated by Emily Chisholm (Oxford: Oxford University Press, 1977). By permission of Oxford University Press, Inc.

Page 103
Prayer: From *Days of the Lord*, vol. 3 (Collegeville, MN: Liturgical Press, 1993). Copyright 1993 by The Order of St. Benedict, Inc. Published by Liturgical Press, Collegeville, Minnesota. Reprinted with permission.

Page 104
Quotation: John Chrysostom, *The Gospel of Matthew*, Homily 87.2.

Page 105
Artwork: Andrea Mantegna (1431–1506), *Calvary*, central predella panel from the St. Zeno of Verona altarpiece, 1456–60 (oil on panel). © Louvre, Paris, France/Lauros/Giraudon/The Bridgeman Art Library.

Page 106
Artwork: *Crucifixion*, from the Rabula Gospels (illuminated manuscript), ca. AD 586. Biblioteca Laurenziana, Florence, Italy. Photo: Scala/Art Resource, NY.

Page 107
Hymn: "Jesus, I Will Ponder Now," public domain.

Page 109
Artwork: French school, *The Descent from the Cross* (ivory group). Musée de Louvre, Paris, France.
Quotation: Peter Chrysologus, Sermon 40. From Joel C. Elowsky, ed., *John 11–21*, Ancient Christian Commentary on Scripture, New Testament, vol. 4b, gen. ed. Thomas C. Oden (Downers Grove, IL: InterVarsity Press, 2007), 324. Used with permission of Augustinian Press. All rights reserved.

Page 110
Artwork: Eustache Le Sueur, *Crucifixion*. Louvre, Paris, France. Photo: Erich Lessing/Art Resource, NY.

Page 113
Artwork: *Crucifixion*, from the Gospels of Countess Judith (England, probably from Canterbury), ca. 1050–65. The Pierpont Morgan Library, New York City, New York. Photo: The Pierpont Morgan Library/Art Resource, NY.
Hymn: "The Royal Banners Forward Go," public domain.

Page 114
Artwork: Master of Westphalia, *Allegory of the Crucifixion*. Copyright © Museo Thyseen-Bornemiaza, Madrid, Spain.

Page 115
Quotation from Ephrem of Syria: From *A Word in Season* © 1981. Reprinted with permission of the Friends of Henry Ashworth, Augustinian Press. All rights reserved.

Page 116
Quotation from Martin Luther: *Sermons on the Gospel of St. John*, p. 375 of vol. 23 of *Luther's Works*, American Edition, © 1959 Concordia Publishing House.

Page 117
Artwork: Giovanni Canavesio (1450–1500), *Crucifixion of Christ*, 1492 (fresco). Chapelle Notre Dame des Fontaines, La Brigue, Alpes Maritimes, France. Photo © François Guenet/Art Resource, NY.
Quotation from Romanos: Reprinted from page 207 of *Kontakia of Romanos, Byzantine Melodist II: On Christian Life* translated and annotated by Marjorie Carpenter, by permission of the University of Missouri Press. Copyright © 1973 by the Curators of the University of Missouri.

Page 118
Artwork: Albrecht Dürer, from *Small Passion*.
Quotation from Martin Luther: Eugene F. A. Klug, ed., *The Complete Sermons of Martin Luther*, vol. 5, trans. Eugene F. A. Klug et al. Copyright © 2000 Baker Books, a division of Baker Publishing Group.

Page 120
Quotation: Leo the Great, Sermon 8.4. From Joel C. Elowsky, ed., *John 11–21*, Ancient Christian Commentary on Scripture, New Testament, vol. 4b, gen. ed. Thomas C. Oden (Downers Grove, IL: InterVarsity Press, 2007), 309. Used with permission of Augustinian Press. All rights reserved.

Page 121
Artwork: Peter Paul Rubens (1577–1640), *The Raising of the Cross*, 1620–21 (sketch for part of the ceiling of the Jesuit church in Antwerp). Louvre, Paris, France. Photo: Erich Lessing/Art Resource, NY.

Page 122
Artwork: Francisco Ribalta, *Nailing to the Cross* (oil on canvas). Photo © The State Hermitage Museum, St. Petersburg, Russia.

Page 124
Hymn: "The Tree of Life," text © 1993 Stephen P. Starke. Administered by Concordia Publishing House.

Page 125
Artwork: Jörg Breu, *The Raising of the Cross*. Szépmüvészeti Múszeum, Budapest, Hungary. Image © Dr. Ron Wiedenhoeft, courtesy of Saskia Ltd.

Page 126
Artwork: Tommaso Masaccio (1401–28), *The Trinity*, 1427–28 (fresco). © Santa Maria Novella, Florence, Italy/The Bridgeman Art Library.

Page 128
Artwork: Hendrik Terbrugghen (1588–1629), *The Crucifixion with the Virgin and Saint John*, ca. 1625 (oil on canvas). The Metropolitan Museum of Art, New York City, New York. Image copyright © The Metropolitan Museum of Art/Art Resource, NY.
Prayer: Collect for Good Friday, *Lutheran Service Book: Altar Book*, © 2006 Concordia Publishing House.

Page 130
Quotation from Martin Luther: Eugene F. A. Klug, ed., *The Complete Sermons of Martin Luther*, vol. 5, trans. Eugene F. A. Klug et al. Copyright © 2000 Baker Books, a division of Baker Publishing Group.

Page 131
Artwork: Parri Spinello (ca. 1387–1453), *Crucifixion*. Palazzo Communale, Arezzo, Italy. Photo: Scala/Art Resource, NY.

Page 132
Artwork: Bonaventura Berlinghieri (1235–74), *Crucifixion*. Pinacoteca Nazionale di Palazzo Mansi, Lucca, Italy. Photo: Scala/Art Resource, NY.

Page 134
Quotation from Romanos: Reprinted from pages 236–37 of *Kontakia of Romanos, Byzantine Melodist I: On the Person of Christ* translated and annotated by Marjorie Carpenter, by permission of the University of Missouri Press. Copyright © 1970 by the Curators of the University of Missouri.

Page 135
Artwork: Giovanni Antonio Pordenone (1484–1539), *Crucifixion*, 1521 (fresco). © Duomo, Cremona, Italy/The Bridgeman Art Library.

Page 136
Artwork: Michelangelo Buonarroti (1475–1564), *Pieta* (marble). © St. Peter's, Vatican, Rome, Italy/The Bridgeman Art Library.

Page 137
Prayer: From *A New Zealand Prayer Book He Karakia Mihinare o Aotearoa*, copyright © 1989 by The Anglican Church in Aotearoa, New Zealand and Polynesia.

Page 138:
Quotation: Michael Marissen, *Lutheranism, Anti-Judaism, and Bach's* St. John Passion (New York: Oxford University Press, 1998), 61. By permission of Oxford University Press, Inc.

Page 139
Artwork: Albrecht Dürer, from *Engraved Passion*.
Quotation: Jerome, Letter 46.3.

Pages 140–41
Artwork: Rogier (Roger) van der Weyden (ca. 1399–1464), *The Crucifixion, with the Virgin and Saint John the Evangelist Mourning*, ca. 1450–55 (oil and gold on panel). John G. Johnson Collection, Philadelphia Museum of Art, Philadelphia, Pennsylvania. Photo: The Philadelphia Museum of Art/Art Resource, NY.

Page 142
Quotation: Walter Wangerin Jr., *The Book of God* (Grand Rapids: Zondervan, 1996), 600–601.

Page 143
Artwork: Mathias Gruenewald (1455–1528), *Crucifixion*, ca. 1515 (limewood; from the Isenheim Altar). Musee d'Unterlinden, Colmar, France. Photo: Erich Lessing/Art Resource, NY.

Page 145
Artwork: Carlo Crivelli (1435/40–93), *Crucifixion*. Pinacoteca di Brera, Milan, Italy. Photo: Scala/Art Resource, NY.
Hymn: "O Sacred Head, Now Wounded," text © 1941 Concordia Publishing House.

Page 146
Quotation in caption: Xavier Bray, "Christ in the Wine Press," in *The Image of Christ*, ed. Gabriele Finaldi (London: National Gallery, 2000), 188.

Page 147
Artwork: Hieronymus Wierix, *Christ in the Wine Press*. British Museum, London, United Kingdom.
Quotation from Clement of Alexandria: From Joan Halmo and Frank Henderson, comp., *Triduum Sourcebook*, vol. 1 (Chicago: Liturgy Training Publications, 1996), 50–51.

Page 148
Artwork: Duccio di Buoninsegna (ca. 1278–1318), *Descent from the Cross*, 1308–11 (from the *Maesta* altarpiece). © Museo dell'Opera del Duomo, Siena, Italy/The Bridgeman Art Library.

Page 149
Quotation from Martin Luther: Eugene F. A. Klug, ed., *The Complete Sermons of Martin Luther*, vol. 5, trans. Eugene F. A. Klug et al. Copyright © 2000 Baker Books, a division of Baker Publishing Group.

Page 150
Poem: Hallgrimur Petursson, *Thirty-one Meditations on Christ's Passion*, trans. Charles V. Pilcher (Bynam, TX: Repristination Press, 2003), 42–43.

Page 151
Artwork: Rhenish school, *Christ on the Cross with Mary and John*, 1450/60. Photo courtesy of Artothek.
Hymn: "Jesus Christ, Our Blessed Savior," public domain.

Page 152
Quotation from Raymond E. Brown: From *A Crucified Christ in Holy Week* (Collegeville, MN: Liturgical Press, 1986). Copyright 1986 by The Order of St. Benedict, Inc. Published by Liturgical Press, Collegeville, Minnesota. Reprinted with permission.
Hymn: "The Royal Banners Forward Go," public domain.

Page 153
Artwork: Francisco de Zurbaran (1598–1664), *Agnus Dei*, ca. 1635–40 (oil on canvas). © Prado, Madrid, Spain/The Bridgeman Art Library.
Quotation from Polycarp of Smyrna: *Patrologia Graeca* 5, 1040. From Costante Berselli, ed., *Hymns to Christ*, trans. Sister Mary of Jesus (Middlegreen, England: St. Paul Publications, 1982). Used with permissions.

Page 154
Artwork: Maerten van Heemskerck, *Golgotha*, 1550. The State Hermitage, St. Petersburg, Russia. Photo courtesy of Artothek.

Pages 156–57
Artwork: Hans Holbein the Younger (1497/8–1543), *The Dead Christ*, 1521 (tempera on panel). © Kunstmuseum, Basel, Switzerland/The Bridgeman Art Library.

Page 157
Quotation: Adamantius (Origen), *Concerning Right Faith in God* 4. From Joel C. Elowsky, ed., *John 11–21*, Ancient Christian Commentary on Scripture, New Testament, vol. 4b, gen. ed. Thomas C. Oden (Downers Grove, IL: InterVarsity Press, 2007), 323.

Page 158
Artwork: Lucas Cranach the Elder, *The Crucifixion with the Converted Centurion*, 1536 (oil on panel). Samuel H. Kress Collection. Image courtesy of the Board of Trustees, National Gallery of Art, Washington DC.

Hymn: "O Darkest Woe," text © Joseph Herl. Used with permission.

Page 159

Hymn: "Christ, the Life of All the Living," public domain.

Quotation from the Augsburg Confession: From *Concordia: The Lutheran Confessions*, second edition; edited by Paul McCain et al., © 2006 Concordia Publishing House.

Page 161

Artwork: Rosso Fiorentino (Giovanni Battista di Jacopo), *The Descent from the Cross*, 1521. Cathedral, Volterra, Italy. Scala. Photo by G. Westermann, Artothek.

Page 162

Artwork: Giovanni Benedetto Castiglione (1609–64), *Crucifixion*. Galleria di Palazzo Bianco, Genoa, Italy. Photo: Scala/Art Resource, NY.

Quotation: From Venantius, *On Easter*.

Hymn text: From "Thy Strong Word," © 1969 Concordia Publishing House.

Page 163

Quotation: Michael Marissen, *Lutheranism, Anti-Judaism, and Bach's* St. John Passion (New York: Oxford University Press, 1998), 64–65. By permission of Oxford University Press, Inc.

Page 164

Artwork: Nicolas Tournier (1590–1638/9), *Christ on the Cross with the Virgin, Mary Magdalene, St. John and St. Francis of Paola* (oil on canvas). © Louvre, Paris, France/Giraudon/The Bridgeman Art Library.

Page 165

Artwork: Pierre-Paul Prud'hon (1758–1823), *Christ on the Cross* (oil on canvas). Louvre, Paris, France. Photo: Réunion des Musées Nationaux/Art Resource, NY.

Page 166

Artwork: Caravaggio (Michelangelo Merisi da) (1573–1610), *The Deposition*, 1600–1604 (oil on canvas). Vatican Museums, Vatican State. Photo: Scala/Art Resource, NY.

Quotation from the Byzantine liturgy: From *Byzantine Daily Worship* © 1969. Published by Alleluia Press, Allendale, New Jersey. Used with permission.

Page 167

Quotation from the Byzantine liturgy: From Sr. Maria, *La Croce nella Preghiera Bizantina* (Brescia, 1979), 88.

Page 168

Prayer: Proper Preface for Holy Week, *Lutheran Service Book: Altar Book*, © 2006 Concordia Publishing House.

Page 169

Artwork: Piero della Francesca (ca. 1415–92), *The Resurrection*, ca. 1463 (fresco). © Pinacoteca, Sansepolcro, Italy/The Bridgeman Art Library.

Quotation from Romanos: Reprinted from page 215 of *Kontakia of Romanos, Byzantine Melodist I: On the Person of Christ* translated and annotated by Marjorie Carpenter, by permission of the University of Missouri Press. Copyright © 1970 by the Curators of the University of Missouri.

Page 170

Artwork: Anastasis, *Christ descending into limbo, saves Adam, Eve, King David, King Solomon*. Monastery Church, Hosios Loukas, Greece. Photo: Erich Lessing/Art Resource, NY.

Hymn: "Upon the Cross Extended," public domain.

Page 172

Artwork: Albrecht Dürer, from *Passio Domini Nostri Jesu per Fratrem Chelidonium Coll.*

Prayer: Collect for Holy Saturday, *Lutheran Service Book: Altar Book*, © 2006 Concordia Publishing House.

Page 173

Hymn: "Awake, My Heart, with Gladness," public domain.

Page 174

Artwork: Jan van Eyck (ca. 1390–1441), *The Adoration of the Lamb*, 1432 (detail from the Ghent Altarpiece). Cathedral of St. Bavo, Ghent, Belgium. Photo: Scala/Art Resource, NY.

Page 175

Quotation from John L. McKenzie: From *The Power and the Wisdom: An Interpretation of The New Testament* (Milwaukee: Bruce, 1965).

Page 176

Quotation from Bo Giertz: From *To Live with Christ*, English translation © 2008 Concordia Publishing House. Used by permission of the Bo Giertz Estate.

Quotation from Martin Luther: From "The Freedom of a Christian," pp. 351–52, in vol. 31 of Luther's Works, American Edition, edited by Harold J. Grimm, copyright © 1957 Augsburg Fortress Press.

Page 177

Artwork: Lucas Cranach the Elder (completed by Lucas Cranach the Younger), Altar der Peter und Paulkirche in Weimar, Germany. Mitteltafel: Christus am Freuz. Weimar, Stadtpfarrkirche. Photo by Constantin Beyer, Artothek.

Page 178

Artwork: Diego Rodriguez de Silva y Velasquez (1599–1660), *Christ on the Cross*, ca. 1630 (oil on canvas). © Prado, Madrid, Spain/The Bridgeman Art Library.

Hymn: "The Royal Banners Forward Go," public domain.

Page 179

Hymn: "Sing, My Tongue, the Glorious Battle," public domain.

Prayer: Proper Preface for Easter, *Lutheran Service Book: Altar Book*, © 2006 Concordia Publishing House.

Page 180

Quotation from John Chrysostom: Adapted from the Pascal Homily, rendered in verse form and attributed to D. Mark Baker; originally accessed at http://www.ocf.org. Available without attribution at www.orthodoxinfo.com/death/resurrection

Page 181

Artwork: Mathias Gruenewald (1455–1528), *Resurrection*, ca. 1515 (limewood; from the Isenheim Altarpiece). Musee d'Unterlinden, Colmar, France. Photo: Erich Lessing/Art Resource, NY.

Pages 182–83

Artwork: The Turin Shroud, ca. 1260–1390 (linen). Cappella della Sacra Sindone, Duomo, Turin, Italy/The Bridgeman Art Library.

Page 183

Hymn: From A. Hammon, ed., *Early Christian Prayers*, trans. Walter Mitchell (London: Longmans, Green, 1961).

Page 185

Artwork: From *The Real Story of the Creation*, © 2007 Concordia Publishing House.

Page 186

Artwork: *Judas Kissing Christ amid Roman Soldiers and Pharisees* (mosaic). S. Marco, Venice, Italy. Photo: Cameraphoto Arte, Venice/Art Resource, NY.